WHEN WE LIVED EAST OF EDEN

Genesis Regenerated–The Bible for the rest of us.

Don Nordstrom

Back to the Desert  Publishing Group

Table of Contents

"One of the saddest lessons of history is this: If we've been bamboozled long enough, we tend to reject any evidence of the bamboozle. We're no longer interested in finding out the truth.

The bamboozle has captured us. It's simply too painful to acknowledge, even to ourselves, that we've been taken. Once you give a charlatan power over you, you almost never get it back."

— Carl Sagan, The Demon-Haunted World: Science as a Candle in the Dark.

Introduction

Mr. Sagan was a brilliant astronomer and scientist.

From this quote in his book, Mr. Sagan allegedly refers to what happens when one replaces science and technology with pseudoscience or religion.

I am guessing he didn't realize the difference between what science, technology, pseudoscience, religion, universities, and governments want us to believe and what the Bible says.

He often implied that science and technology were the world's savior, not pseudoscience or religion. It is agreed that science and technology have given us significant innovations and, sometimes, improved our quality of life. However, it has also brought destruction to our world and our lives—think military weapons, toxic chemicals, alleged GMOs, pollution, and other detrimental activities.

In the same tone, religion has brought a unifying belief in God, yet divided people into around 30,000 religions with different doctrines, each claiming to be the true religion, yet all are bamboozled.

This might sound strange at first, coming from a born-again, fire-baptized disciple of Jesus, but we will see how religions have tricked their members.

This book you are about to read will show us we've all been bamboozled, or what we would call deceived or tricked. We are all ignorant, to a degree, and most choose to stay that way.

Ignorance means we don't know any better. However, if we learn differently or the truth, but decide to remain ignorant, we could become stupid and be enslaved to others, at least as far as what they tell us to believe.

The deceptions begin when we start learning.

See, our brain holds a giant memory vault. It doesn't care what we put in there. There could be lies, deception, facts, or truth. It doesn't know the difference. However, we have something called a soul to help us sort things out.

We all learn from an academic paradigm in life and school. This means we learn from a pre-designed structure, each comprising channels of thought and learning. Sure, we all know what people take as fact, such as $2 + 2 = 4$, or the sky is blue. But what color is the sky at night?

However, within these academic paradigms of learning are hearsay, opinion, assumption, tradition, and error. We might learn from history what others believed and taught, and it has passed down into schools of learning, whether secular or Bible schools.

The religious channels would teach creation, as God created everything in Genesis chapter 1. The scientific channels, as macro-evolutionists, teach there is no God and all things exist by happenstance or survival of the fittest. Somehow, everything could adapt or create what it needed to survive before extinction.

To ensure their teaching doesn't stray far from their academic paradigms, a religious scholar may ignore it when perhaps evidence shows our earth is millions of years old and might prove the scientist correct. Just as when an evolutionary scientist stumbles across a finding that might prove, at a minimum, intelligent design, they ignore it. From these two arguments, they will never end.

We will discover the followers of both channels, science and religion, have been bamboozled about the creation story in the Bible or perhaps why our earth appears millions of years old.

No matter what academic paradigm we've learned from, each group should step out of their boxes and consider a third alternative: We may have been taught the wrong creation story from the Bible.

If this is true, and we will prove it is, we can discover that neither group is right or wrong. It all depends on whether we are using our own or God's perspectives.

Admittedly, this book is probably dead on arrival for our atheist acquaintances since they "know" there is no God. Again, try this book and see why people don't believe there is God—how they've been bamboozled, like the religious groups have been about God's creation. Try to absorb the painful knowledge that we've been tricked and then be set free forever.

Consider for a few moments how we've been deceived into believing what Bible teachers have taught us for centuries: that Genesis 1:1 is showing us our universe and earth were created in the first verse, or, "In the beginning, God created the heaven and earth."

Hmm…, it seems simple enough—so what is the argument? It is this. God isn't telling us something from the beginning of our physical realm or time. He tells us HIS story from the start or establishment of His kingdom, from His spiritual realm.

Does this mean there is a spiritual realm, God, and He has His own separate heaven and earth? Yep, because the Bible and God say He does, and through something called Binary Effects, we will prove it to the atheists, creation scientists, and Bible teachers as well.

We've never learned the rest of the story about His creation, which the Bible tells us in other places. We've never made the connections back to Genesis 1.

First, this book summarizes a hard-to-believe story. Through building foundations, we will slowly understand the alternative creation story. It is all there in Genesis, right before our eyes. Religious teachers have blocked it from us, and we've read it with preconceived ideas.

We will see we've often skipped over three words, thinking they meant the same thing, but they did not, with other entries that prove Genesis 1 is not the creation of our heaven and earth or all things-yet.

God did not create everything in the first chapter, as it shows many things were already created.

Bible teachers never explained, with any reasoning, the meaning of other verses in the following Genesis chapters concerning the creation. They taught the verses were in chronological order after chapter 1. Instead, they reflect on Genesis 1.

One key to understanding the creation story is it is given from two spiritual perspectives: God and the Lord God. When the narrative is coming from or about God, it is describing His heaven and earth. The Lord God conducts His teaching as establishing what will become our earth and heavens-universe.

In addition, none of it is taking place in our physical realm, but is directed from God's spirit realm. Our physical realm begins after the judgment in Genesis 7.

Therefore, please read along with our bamboozled atheists and religious believers and prepare to go through the pain of learning the bamboozle, and choose to be set free from our history of creation deceptions. Get ready to wake up and get personal with our creator and maker. He will show us His creation story from heaven.

In The Beginning ... ?

Deception is a powerful tool. It's been used since before the beginning of time. Deception works by first stating something we might know as fact and then saying something that isn't completely true or not at all. Once the fact has been established in our minds, what follows is also a fact.

It was previously mentioned that 2+2=4, probably a fact, but also stated the sky is blue, which it isn't. It only appears blue in the daytime from the sun's rays hitting our atmosphere.

This brings up another deception. There is no literal sky, just different layers of atmosphere. Sometimes we've called it heaven, which it isn't. What else have we been told in deception? Plenty, especially from tradition and education, including science, government, and the Bible. This could make a whole different book, but we are here to learn the alternate creation story.

We've read through the Genesis creation with preconceived beliefs. This has presented conflicts of interpretation. The opening words of the Bible state, "In the beginning." What does in the beginning mean?

We will look at the alternate structure of the beginning chapters of Genesis. From this, we will better understand the creation, the Bible, and our lives. We will reveal why we are here, how we got here, and where we are going for eternity.

Genesis' creation is like the foundation of the Bible. If we get the beginning or premise wrong, we won't understand or believe in the Bible, at least from what we consider it to be teaching us.

This is one reason why there is so much argument between creationists, religions, and those who don't believe in the Bible. Some think the Bible presents more questions than answers because we have never learned what the creation story is telling us.

What if the Bible doesn't say God created everything in Genesis 1? What if we've missed simple observations that prove God is not revealing our current heaven-universe and earth?

From Bible history, religious doctrines have taught us that Genesis 1 is God telling us He created our heaven or universe, earth, space, and time from nothing in six twenty-four days—some say twelve-hour days.

Secular history teaches evolutionary thought started or at least blossomed in the 19th century, promoting uniformity or slow change over millions of years, which has always governed our existence, ignoring cataclysmic events and obvious genetic mutations or transference to form other like-kind organisms.

We will try to get both avenues of these academic paradigms to take a fresh look at the first chapters of Genesis from an alternative structure to what we learned. Let this different viewpoint from Genesis and the Bible begin with an overview.

What is the beginning or creation? Are they the first three verses in Genesis 1? Is it the entire chapter? Or does it also include Chapter 2?

We will learn the creation story is told through Genesis chapters 1–8, and discover these chapters are like a cycle or point back to Genesis 1. Numerous verses in the Bible reflect back to the beginning, even in the Book of Revelation.

We need to read Genesis chapters 2–8 to understand chapter 1.

Various people who read the first three verses of Genesis 1 believe in the Gap Theory, when there may be eons of time between the first three verses. In other words, our current earth may have existed for a long time, and it took eons of destruction from fallen angels and Lucifer to make our earth "without form and void."

This version started when certain scientists began "proving" our universe is billions of years old. Therefore, according to Jewish genealogy, our earth is approximately 6,000 years old; it had to be much older.

Certain creation teachers had to develop an extended story to accommodate the old earth theory.

This book is not a rehash of this gap theory or belief since it isn't complete and out of order.

However, it is somewhat correct, and the adaptive science theory is partially correct.

Let's take the gap theory as presently taught. It implies our physical earth was at one time perfect before it deteriorated into a "without form and void" giant blob of darkened waters (Genesis 1:2). Or, as a deceived Bible teacher might state, "God created our earth that way."

But what we will see is that our current earth was never perfect and is the by-product, so to speak, of God's perfect earth or kingdom. It is God's earth that became without form and void into darkened waters. Here is the basis for God's alternate creation version presented in this book.

The creation story is a spiritual story about God's kingdom. It isn't referring to our current earth until much later.

God is speaking of "in the beginning" as the start of a story—His story, not our story or the creation of our universe. There are three things we will discover.

One is, in Genesis 1:1–3, the story begins with the creation of His kingdom heaven and earth in His eternity past spirit realm—its almost total destruction, its restoration, and it does not occur in our physical realm.

Two: Genesis chapter 1 is a summary statement and introduction for the rest of the story, starting from verse one. In other words, what we discover in Genesis chapters 2–8 is why Genesis 1 happened and why His earth became without form and void, or separated from God's restored earth.

Three: We were initially formed as an eternal living soul in a spirit body before becoming physically alive on our earth. We first existed in the spirit realm, east of Eden. Everyone has an eternal spirit and soul, currently encapsulated by a physical body, because we are temporarily here in our physical realm.

This is the beginning of the hard-to-believe story. It will later be shown from the Bible and through our existence how we prove this version of the creation story.

The beginning is when God created His earth in His heaven, or spirit realm. It means our physical heaven and earth came later from this "without form and void" spiritual earth. Our universe-heavens and earth are later "made" or pre-made in the spiritual realm.

In the rest of Genesis chapter 1, God restores a new heaven and earth for eternity in His realm, and the Lord God makes a temporary realm for us starting in Chapter 2:4.

God divides His "without form and void" earth, which has become dark waters, first into His restored earth. With the leftover remnants, the Lord God, in parallel, makes what will become our destructed universe and earth. God uses something called a firmament to accomplish this task.

Initially, it might sound strange to know our universe and earth came from God's destructed earth from a different universe or realm. It will make more sense the deeper we get into the story.

In addition, we will learn about binary, which God used a form of in His word to help us understand Him, Genesis, and in the replication of our lives and environment to prove His existence to us. We will see when Solomon, perhaps the wisest person ever, spoke about how

God's binary effects now govern our world, which proves His existence.

Instead of repeating traditional creation teachings or a Gap theory from a physical, human perspective, this book tries to see Genesis' creation and the Bible from God's wisdom, His story, from His realm. We will find other Bible verses that scholars and others have had difficulty understanding, will suddenly support this alternate story.

A person may find this version even more difficult to believe and can certainly reject it and stick to the Genesis teachings handed down, primarily through hearsay—or look at the creation in Genesis in a whole new way, through the eyes of the inspiring author of the Bible, God.

This book provides more answers than questions. God often reflects and reveals what happened in His world and how it occurs throughout our lives. The operative is: He daily shows us throughout our lives what happened in His realm and why we are here.

We consistently experience it, and yet we don't realize it is all in front of us each day.

To understand this book's themes, we must first know there is a spiritual and separate physical realm where we now temporarily exist. Our temporary physical realm came from God's eternal spirit realm.

God does not physically exist here, but spiritually in His kingdom and with His Spirit in the born-again, fire-baptized Christians stemming from the day of Pentecost, when Jesus' disciples first, internally, received His Spirit.

This is the true church through spiritual baptism, bypassing religions, and being transferred into true Christians throughout the centuries until today. We will discover, these are the true Christians or disciples of Jesus' "church".

For now, consider the spiritual realm as a separate universe. We will do a bit of spiritual and scientific reckoning to show this is true.

Before we begin, we have to go through a brief Bible and foundational study to develop our base of understanding so we can realize what we read is within our grasp of learning.

Why what comes next isn't taught in churches is unclear. We shouldn't have to struggle to understand the Bible from unspiritual religious teachers.

There had to be a different answer. There is, and we will get a whole new spiritual perspective on the creation than what we've been taught. Prepare to learn the Bible for the rest of us.

Brief Bible Study

We have to interrupt our journey momentarily to learn more about our Bible. This will be a brief, foundational background, which I wish I had received from the dozens of churches I attended or the thousands of sermons I had heard over the decades. We must dissolve a few misconceptions or deceptions that block our spiritual understanding of God and the Bible.

Various people believe the Bible is a book of fables, perhaps because no one can answer their tough questions. For example:

Was there a talking serpent, cherubs, or a flaming sword in Eden?

Did Balaam's donkey talk?

Had Jonah survived for three days and nights inside a whale?

Can a burning bush speak?

Was the sun stuck for days when Joshua was in battle?

In a moment, we will determine yes or no, and if so, how and why.

The Bible most people use today has two parts: the Old Testament (OT) and the New Testament (NT). It is a library of sixty-six books. These testaments are documented covenants developed first between God and the Jewish people, and later, including the non-Jews or Gentiles.[1]

---

[1] The terms Jews or Jewish probably didn't occur until the tribe of Judah. The book uses these terms throughout to describe the Hebrew people.

A few people think Bible writers first wrote the Bible in English. The Jews first wrote it in Hebrew and Aramaic, and later, Greek translators wrote the OT in Greek as the Septuagint and later, the NT. The Middle English translations started around the 14th century AD.

There are places where the Bible speaks about the non-Jews or Gentiles existing with the Jewish people and their relationship to the Jewish populations and their God.

I the LORD have called thee in righteousness, and will hold thine hand, and will keep thee, and give thee for a covenant of the people, for a light of the Gentiles;

To open the blind eyes, to bring out the prisoners from the prison, and them that sit in darkness out of the prison house.

–Isaiah 42:6-7

However, God inspired the Bible to the Jews, by the Jews, and for the Jews. Religions may try to convert historical events for the Jews as doctrines to control our lives today, when they are false.

In the eleventh chapter of Genesis, we are introduced to a guy named Abram. God unconditionally bound the Jewish people to Him by the old covenant through Abram; his name was later changed to Abraham to show the covenant made between him and God.

Later, the Jewish people chose their allegiance to God through the Mosaic laws, or the Ten Commandments. The commandments showed the standard or righteousness of God, and because no one could achieve this standard, we all needed a savior. The relationship between God and people has always been interpersonal, without interference or obstacles from any religion or organization.

The Abrahamic covenant was not conditional, as promised to the Jewish people, meaning neither God nor people could break this covenant. The covenant given to Moses was conditional and had to be chosen and accepted by the people. If the Jews broke any of the laws on purpose, they would suffer the consequences.

The Jews were supposed to recognize their Messiah or Savior promised in the OT and later choose to be bound by the NT covenant through Yeshua (Hebrew) or Jesus (Greek).

Unfortunately, the Jewish leadership did/does not do this, so God also made the NT covenant available to the Gentiles or non-Jews.

What made these covenants unique was the blood shed in fulfilling them. Priests would sacrifice clean animals on an altar, which temporarily covered the sins of the people.

Jesus' shed blood on an altar or cross permanently erased our sins. This covering and removing of sins is the distinction between the old and new covenants.

The Jewish disciples of Jesus and their followers were the first to receive the Spirit of God in their spirit at Pentecost. Later, Paul introduced the gospel of Jesus to the Gentiles, and they also received the same Spirit from God. We can still receive this spirit immersion today, which differs from water baptism.

The OT is much thicker because it establishes the reason for the NT. However, the OT is closed, the NT will exist for eternity, and the Bible is now complete.

The OT spiritually ended at Pentecost in approximately AD 33. However, the Jewish priests continued their animal sacrifices until about AD 66, when the Romans started their assault on Jerusalem, and forever after the destruction of the temple, through 70 AD.

This almost total destruction of Jerusalem, the temple mount, Israel, and the slaughter of Roman soldiers, Syrians, Arabs, and Idumeans from surrounding nations, along with Zealots and innumerable Jewish people, was called Armageddon.

After the 70 AD devastation is the end of physical history in the New Testament, described as a coming prophecy in the Book of Revelation to Israel as a warning about their coming destruction. The NT ending in Revelation includes the release of the kingdom of God into spirit-baptized Christians.

Of course, hundreds of people have made tons of money trying to deceive and tweak the Books of Daniel and Revelation concerning our end times.

But we still need the OT as a historical reference, as the NT writers and Jesus referred to it, and we can look up what they meant in their writings. We sometimes need to know the history.

For example, since Jesus mentioned Abel and Noah, we can depend on them and know they truly existed during the creation. Jesus also encountered the devil and his demons. They exist on our earth, or Jesus was a liar, and we need not go further.

As a non-Jewish person, we can thank God and the Jewish people for bringing the new covenant to us. This means we can adopt the promises from the new covenant if we aren't Jewish—just not the religion-created false doctrines.

Another important thing we need to know to understand the Bible better is it mainly pertains to an area of land chosen by God to be His part of our planet. We know this land as Israel.

Then will I pluck them up by the roots out of my land which I have given them;

–2 Chronicles 7:20

Often, God will speak of this part of the earth as the world, not to be confused with our planet Earth. It was His home away from home on our earth to interact with His spiritual wife, the Jewish people.

For the Lord hath called thee as a woman forsaken and grieved in spirit, and a wife of youth, when thou wast refused, saith thy God.

–Isaiah 54:6

In addition, the world or nations in the Bible are often referred to as the lands immediately surrounding Israel and not the nations on the rest of the planet. Besides, no other country or people outside of the immediate nations surrounding Israel would have known about God.

These other outer nations were governed by false gods or fallen angels as demons and still are today, which often infiltrated the nations as idols surrounding Israel. People crafted these idols to represent the fallen angels.

Knowing these things as the basis for a Bible study and soon knowing about binary will make many scripture verses stand out or be spiritually clearer. God often reveals what happened in His world through the Jewish people and our lives. The Bible consistently draws us into His spirit-realm kingdom.

Some Bible teachers think the whole Bible is literal when it is not. The Jewish writers often used symbolism or an idiom, a type of figure of speech.

They sometimes used symbolism in prose, such as a beast, meaning an evil ruler or king.

Knowing a bit of Bible history helps us better understand what is said and meant. Who is doing the writing, and to whom? Where is the writing taking place? Other times, we need to know when God is revealing His spirit in His, or our world or earth, Israel, and the nations surrounding Jerusalem. Therefore, knowing the context of verses is extremely important.

From this, we can better understand the previously presented troublesome questions.

1. Talking serpent? Since the Garden of Eden was in God's kingdom and thus in His world, yes, there was a talking serpent, cherubs, and a flaming sword.

2. Talking donkey? Balaam's donkey, and later, Balaam, had a spiritual experience with an angel of the Lord (Numbers 22:22–34). His donkey first saw the angel with a sword blocking their way, and the donkey turned so as not to get killed.

Balaam started beating the donkey, and the angel caused the donkey to speak to Balaam, who then also saw the angel. The angel from the spirit realm caused the donkey to speak.

Angels are messengers who come from the spirit realm and deliver warnings or perform what we call miracles, such as a talking donkey.

3. Was Jonah swallowed by a whale? God told Jonah to preach to the pagans in the city of Nineveh, who were extremely evil.

Supposedly, the Ninevites would pull their slaves around with fish hooks because they worshiped a fish god named Dagon, as did many others. God told Jonah to preach to Nineveh; instead, he was afraid and tried to escape on a boat.

The verses in Jonah, chapter 1, say the Lord "prepared" or anointed a great fish, not a whale, to swallow Jonah. It was probably a whale shark, which is a fish with an enormous mouth.

At any rate, it appears the Lord adapted the fish, or the fish gulped a considerable amount of oxygen along with Jonah.

But the scripture also implies Jonah entered into a coma in the fish, which may have prolonged his life, and then resurrected on the shore when the fish vomited him out.

The pagans of Nineveh started listening to Jonah, as he probably appeared as Dagon, their fish god, coming alive to them.

4. Talking bush? Whether there was an actual burning bush, such as from a eucalyptus plant on fire, or the Lord took on the physical element of fire to speak to Moses, it was also an interaction from the spirit realm. Many people today still have spiritual experiences, especially concerning their conversion to becoming disciples of Jesus.

5. The sun stood still? As far as the sun literally standing still for Joshua and his armies, it is most likely a misunderstanding.

For one thing, we know the earth revolves around the sun, so if it happened, the scripture would have read, "The earth stood still, so the sun stood still."

Of course, the Biblically illiterate Roman religion almost had Galileo killed because this verse showed them the sun revolved around the earth and stopped, when, instead, he argued the earth revolved around the sun.

Joshua was either describing the summer solstice (solstice means sun-still), when the sun seems to stay in its northernmost position for a few days.

Or, it was a type of idiom or figure of speech when someone displays an impressive ability that lasts for a duration.

For example:

Let's say a major league ballplayer hits four home runs in a game. The announcer might say, "The sun certainly kept shining on him." This would be an idiom from today.

Therefore, this is most likely what the Bible means when it says:

Then spake Joshua to the Lord in the day when the Lord delivered up the Amorites before the children of Israel, and he said in the sight of Israel, Sun, stand thou still upon Gibeon; and thou, Moon, in the valley of Ajalon.

And the sun stood still, and the moon stayed, until the people had avenged themselves upon their enemies.

Is not this written in the book of Jasher? So the sun stood still in the midst of heaven, and hasted not to go down about a whole day.

And there was no day like that before it or after it, that the Lord hearkened unto the voice of a man: for the Lord fought for Israel.

–Joshua 10:12-14

The sun and moon symbolized the staying power of the Lord with Joshua and stayed with them day and night until Joshua and his army avenged their enemies because the Lord consistently fought for them, not because the sun and moon stood still. We see the same 'sun' idiom used in the book of Ephesians 4:25–26:

Wherefore putting away lying, speak every man truth with his neighbour: for we are members one of another.

Be ye angry, and sin not: let not the sun go down upon your wrath:

Neither give place to the devil.

These verses say to stay angry against the devil, or the devil will control your life through lies and sin.

There are many things we might not understand initially from the Bible until we realize the scripture was for the Jews during their lifetimes. We often need to adjust our thinking to their culture. We will see God's word clearer by asking Him to reveal the scriptures to us.

Can we use other tools to understand the Bible and an alternate creation story? Yes, they are The Binary Effects of God. God used a form of binary in the Bible and in our lives to prove His existence to us through images or binary effects.

It sounds "sciencey," but it isn't. It is the basis for everything. Let's find out!

I m a g e s

Images are powerful. We could describe an object with four wheels, a metallic and plastic body, an engine, windows, doors, a steering wheel, and other parts, or simply show an image of a car.

By seeing the image, we would know instantly without description what it is, generally how it is made, what it does, what it is used for, and so forth. Everything we see as an image is a collection of something else from a process in time.

Images can also protect us. For example, we could watch a program where a hydrogen bomb explodes. We would be instantly vaporized if we stood in its presence as it went off.

God uses images, which are processed from His realm. He is temporarily separating us from Him through images so we won't be immediately transcended back into darkness or darkness-waters from Genesis 1:2, and so we could no longer rebel against Him in His kingdom.

We are here on our earth, in the physical realm, with our spiritual soul and body enclosed in a physical body, with physical images consistently revealing events from God's kingdom.

When we gaze out at our universe at night from our earth, we see the image of His destructed 'without form and void' earth. Time is ticking out how long our sentence is for helping destroy His earth. Hold that thought for now.

Part of the problem with viewing an image is we cannot see what is inside of it. An X-ray can show us some of the inner workings of our body, but not everything, including our spirit and soul.

We would have to disassemble the car to see what is in it, but still not see everything.

Approximately twenty-five years ago, I was in a spiritual valley. Many true Christians sometimes go through these desperate times when, for one reason or another, God doesn't make His presence known to us, perhaps for years. The Psalmist, David, wrote several Psalms concerning the same thing. [2]

One day, I was frustrated and fed up with not hearing from God. So I did what perhaps every repentant, born-again, fire-baptized disciple of Jesus does. I laid out face down on my living room floor and threw a world-class spiritual tantrum.

I told God I wasn't putting up with His silence until he started proving His presence to me again. Be careful how you behave and what you request from God. I am sure He wasn't impressed with my tantrum, but that I humbled myself by lying prostrate face down before Him.

At some point, He stopped my tantrum, probably before I would have a heart attack or stroke. He must have told me to grab a notebook and a pen, sit at the dining room table, and write what He would show me. It was the last thing I physically remembered for the next seven days.

I must have eaten food, gone to the bathroom, ventured outside, slept, and so forth, but I didn't remember any of it. What God did was control my actions and somehow stick a spiritual firehose in my brain, non-stop, for a week.

When God gave me my 7-day firehose spiritual education, my experience came as living images. It took seven days to show me all He intended.

---

[2] Psalm 13:1–5, Psalm 22:1–2

I remembered the images given to me were in something like 3D movies on sections of tapestries, or the tapestries were the images showing the movies. It didn't matter.

Each section of the movie-tapestry would blend spiritually with the rest of the movie sections on that material and into other tapestries behind it, which I could see through the first tapestry. I could see through images.

I could watch one movie, and it would transfer to another movie playing on the same fabric or pass through to a movie in a different tapestry, binding them with the other tapestries or with other sections, which explained the previous images.

When the experience started, it was not clear what the first images meant. However, as the rest came, I realized I was passing through and learning the images, and then understood the previous ones. In the end, and with my notes, the images were mostly understandable. However, they were mind-boggling and difficult to believe.

It took a long time for them to blend into my mind. Although I didn't immediately translate all the meanings, I understood more throughout the years. It took that long to remove all the religious garbage I had collected through the decades. Once I interpreted the spiritual meaning behind the images, I found the courage to write this book, challenging the religious teachings on creation.

The primary message revealed is, we do not understand how deceived we are in all our lives. We've been cast into and exist in a world full of deception. Everything has become a deception in one way or another, and we are bamboozled into believing them.

The destruction of us and humanity before we receive God's eternal plan of salvation is the devil's goal, and our planet is his playground. His illusions have engulfed us for thousands of years. However, everything is from God, but the devil has twisted it all into deceiving us.

And the great dragon was cast out, that old serpent, called the Devil, and Satan, which deceiveth the whole world:

he was cast out into the earth, and his angels were cast out with him.

–Revelation 12:9

We don't know why we are here, where we came from, or where we are going. However, the answers are in our faces every day.

To help us understand this verse from the Book of Revelation, the Apostle John sees spiritual images of what will happen to Israel, Jerusalem, and their temple and why their destruction is coming.

He can pierce within images from ages past, the spiritual reasons the Jewish destruction occurred between approximately AD 66-70. This Revelation verse occurred perhaps eons ago, or why God's earth was 'without form and void'.

Notice this Revelation scripture says, "deceiveth the whole world". There are no exclusions or exceptions. As mentioned, the answers were mind-boggling, and this was just one of many.

I know many readers may think I am leading them down a rabbit hole and that I am the bamboozled one. However, the more light shown in the darkness of deception, the better readers will believe the alternate creation story.

Throughout the years, the real deal was, how could I show this to others so they could also see and understand? The answer came from the Binary Effects of God. From this, God showed me how to set the foundation of everything through binary images.

When God came to our earth, He arrived in the physical image of Yeshua, or Jesus. If he had come as almighty God without a physical body, everyone in His presence would have been instantly vaporized because of our intentional sins.

The physical image of Jesus protected those in His presence and soon contained the Spirit of God within, after His Spirit baptism. We can receive the same baptism in our spirit.

We all exist in a temporary image of a physical body containing our spirit and soul. The Spirit of God comes into our spirit when we are born again in the fire baptism from Pentecost.

After we receive this eternal baptism, we can see, like John did, into the spirit realm. We can find answers for, 'Why did God make our universe and earth and place me here? What is the point of everything'?

Our physical body allows us to function in our physical realm. When we die, our physical body dissolves, and our spirit and soul take over in the eternal spirit realm. Our eternal spirit soul allows us to exist in the spirit realm forever, just as our physical body enables us to function in the temporary physical realm.

And the very God of peace sanctify you wholly; and I pray God your whole spirit and soul and body be preserved blameless unto the coming of our Lord Jesus Christ.

–1 Thessalonians 5:23

Another thing I learned is that everything in the spirit world is transparent, or we see through the images. There are no hidden agendas or deceptions. This is difficult to say because we can see everything from beginning to end in the spirit realm, yet there is no beginning or end in God's kingdom. We can experience everything at once.

Remember the former things of old: for I am God, and there is none else; I am God, and there is none like me,

Declaring the end from the beginning, and from ancient times the things that are not yet done, saying, My counsel shall stand, and I will do all my pleasure:

–Isaiah 46:9-10

These are just a couple of verses that reflect the creation. The edict in eternity was to create and restore forever. We experience these ancient times each day of our lives, or are shown why we are here.

On our earth, we can see a tree, but only the bark on the outside, unless we cut into it. Smaller items are inside besides the finely grained wood, down to molecules and more. We cannot see microscopic items with just our eyes that make up the inner part of the tree.

The table I sat at while taking notes during my seven-day spiritual experience was a bunch of floating molecules from a tree. The image changed and was fixed together to form a complex, molecular, hard table.

What we see as an image of words in the Bible often has more profound spiritual meanings within the words. We will see what Jesus called it—hidden manna. Sometimes we need to read other chapters before we can see through the image of something previously presented.

After my experience, I knew God created everything through His word into images for us. Everything of substance is an image of a larger spiritual picture from the Word of God. Images often have additional visions within.

The tough part is to turn those images back into spiritual words and get people to see and understand the visions given to us are to prove that God exists in His kingdom. He often reveals His history to us. Is that a compound word from God to us: His-story?

What God has done to prove His existence to us in our world is that He left us with His effects as images of what we will discover are His binary effects. We may not see the wind blow, but we know how it affects trees and our hair. When we change our physical perspective to spiritual, like seeing inside or at least knowing it is there, we can understand His images.

Symbols or symbolism, an allegory or metaphor, can also be a spiritual image. We find these throughout the Bible, especially in the Book of Revelation. Once people understand the spiritual images of symbolism, they can easily see the Revelation story arises from the OT symbols of warning to the Jewish people.

What is about to be shown is easily understandable. We will see how God used His binary effects of images in His Bible and our world so we can understand the creation story.

The Binary Effects of God

Our eagerness to explore Genesis and its alternative creation structure is understood. However, please be patient for a little longer, as we will soon see God showing us what He went through during the destruction and restoration of His kingdom.

We first understand binary, developed through a numbering system.

We all know the decimal system of multiple tens or times ten: 0, 1, 10, 100, 1000, and so on. Zero is the launch pad from nothing, as it starts with a 1, or something.

Binary is similar, starting with 0 and 1, but doubling or twice the result. From this, we can develop a binary numbering system starting from 0:

$1 \times 2 = 2$

$2 \times 2 = 4$

$4 \times 2 = 8$

$8 \times 2 = 16$, and so on.

This binary numbering system doesn't go beyond our scope here. It shows how we first started using binary as a basis of two, or 0-1, nothing, and something.

However, within this image of 2, we could also expand binary into many other things. As a result, we will see something that becomes a product of binary or a binary effect from God.

The first image duality of binary becomes evident in the beginning of Genesis as an image of heaven and earth. It is in everything.

If I could write on a whiteboard a 0 and a 1, along with a picture of a box, and tell the audience that if I could place this 0 and 1 into the box, and presto-chango, turn it into a computer or smartphone, the audience, other than computer coders, would probably laugh their heads off.

Yet, to further explain binary and how we can use it today, if readers are using a computer or smartphone to read this from an eBook, its primary function is based on binary, along with, as a result, everything else. We don't see binary working on the surface unless we look deeper into the images.

The next example is:

Let's say there is a dark dot.

●

It has a value of zero or 0 or nothing.

Now, if the dot is lit:

1

It has a value of one, 1, or something.

If we can keep this idea of nothing and something, or darkness and light, opposites in our minds, it will help guide us to understanding the creation and restoration. These dots are opposite of each other, off or on. We can expand these linked, oppositional images into almost everything, including dead or living.

Ever wonder why there is an off-on? How about the contrasts between dark and light, north and south, east and west, up and down, old and new, water and land, heaven and earth, or the spiritual and physical realms? Once we understand this opposite type of linked existence, if there is a physical realm, there must be a spiritual realm!

There is another function where we could keep changing these dots back and forth or repeatedly turn something off, to on, to off, to on.

An extreme speed of switching laser light off and on is how light works in fiber optics to transmit information.

Also, consider something that was new at one time. However, it eventually became old or corrupted and was restored to be new again. These are a few of the Binary Effects of God.

Light to Dark to Light

It is possible we could not fully understand the beginning of Genesis until God released His binary effects wisdom to us.

Now, let's look at Genesis 1 from this alternative viewpoint.

In the beginning, God created the heaven and the earth. And the earth was without form, and void; and darkness was upon the face of the deep. And the Spirit of God moved upon the face of the waters.

And God said, Let there be light: and there was light.

–Genesis 1:1-3

At first glance, we may not see the binary effects. We could interpret there was something already in existence in the spirit realm eons ago, heaven and earth, in the past tense as the start of a story.

What it doesn't immediately show us is there was light before the darkness on the face of the deep. Part of the deception taught to us is God created our earth without form and void, in darkness. In verse three, He created light. However, it doesn't say created; it says let.

In order to know darkness, there first has to be light. We find other scriptures that displace religious deceptions.

This then is the message which we have heard of him, and declare unto you, that God is light, and in him is no darkness at all.

–1 John 1:5

In order to have darkness, there had to first be light. This implies that the earth was also light before darkness because there was always light in heaven, from God, who is eternal.

The only creation we can take from these first verses is that God created heaven and earth. It doesn't say He created the earth without form and void, or in darkness. We miss the image change in the scene.

Our first image is God created heaven and earth. In the second image, the earth is without form and void in the darkness of the waters, and in the third, the Spirit of God moves upon the face of the waters.

What is missing are the details of what happened between the created heaven and earth, to the without form and void earth in darkness, and to the Spirit of God on the face of the waters. We haven't learned yet that what is missing is explained in better detail in Genesis chapters 2–8!

These Genesis chapters show us how the Lord God made an earth from a without form and void earth, and how it turned into our current earth. The Lord God made this earth to restore God's kingdom and to show how God's earth became without form and void. This is spiritually cyclic, and although we might not know it at this moment, is how our physical realm functions.

Genesis chapter 1 shows us part of this destructed earth, land, and seas is restored to something new, or brought back into light, with the Spirit of God moving upon the waters.

These are the binary effects of creation, destruction, and restoration—the result of binary into trinary.

Since God is eternal, He has always been light, and so was His kingdom until darkness came against Him.

Therefore, something happened externally, as the darkness on the face of the deep or the eternal realm, as Genesis chapters 2–8 will show us.

Let's look at the beginning of the story again with our new understanding of binary.

"In the beginning, God created the heaven and the earth." (Creation in binary as heaven and earth). "And the earth was without form and void; and darkness was upon the face of the deep." Without form and void with darkness (Decreation of creation), a binary effect of creation.

"And the Spirit of God moved upon the face of the waters." (Restoration binary from the decreation from darkness-waters). Can we see this as binary into trinary or trinity coming from a trinary God?

Earth is a binary effect of heaven. Without form and void with darkness on the deep is a binary effect from creating earth in the light of heaven. The Spirit moving on the face of the darkened waters is a restoration; a binary effect from darkened waters of a without form and void earth.

Is there something else God is trying to show us? What if these first verses, seeing binary and trinity, are a summary statement or image of the Theory of Everything from God? Creation, decreation, and restoration.

It becomes a persistent cycle or revolving as an orb or sphere of reaction from the action of creation. And the best thing is, He reveals His creation story to us every day.

Ever wonder why our earth, planets, and stars are in an orb or sphere and revolve around something else? On our planet, we daily experience light to dark, restored to light again as a new day, just as in the beginning. Images from God!

Again, these are images for us from God to show what happened in His kingdom in His spiritual realm, teaching us by revolving His images daily throughout our lives. We observe everything as a reaction to the actions of God in binary images. Our physical realm is a reaction from actions in the spiritual realm.

We can now see these images as God reveals His "In the beginning..." spiritual events to us daily.

The Bible describes an OLD covenant and a NEW covenant, or Testaments, a binary effect of the Bible. How many times have we looked at a Bible and never saw this?

The word of God oozes out of the Old and New Testaments, or Bible, into our hearts and minds through His Spirit, creating His binary images for us.

The old becomes new to restore us to His kingdom, just like in Genesis chapter 1, where He is restoring His kingdom from the darkness-waters.

He reveals to us through His word and binary images what happened in His spiritual kingdom and what He is doing to restore us to Him.

We are stepping out of the old creation box, whether or not we know it.

It has been preconceived in our minds through the flawed religious doctrine that Genesis chapter 1 is the creation of our heaven and earth. However, God first shows us His earth in His heaven, or spirit realm.

This begs the question: What is the first chapter of Genesis teaching us?

First, we must get rid of our ancient, arrogant thinking. If we instead look at the Bible and our lives and environment as God constantly revealing in His word and images in our physical world, His nature, and what happened in His spiritual world, the Bible and our lives come alive with more profound meaning and spiritual inspiration.

Millions of learned people know the Bible scriptures, but few understand the spiritual images presented. There is a big difference as far as the east is from the west. As God finished the Genesis Chapter 1 restoration of His Spirit realm, He assured us all is very good again in His kingdom.

Religious teachers taught us to read the Bible through our paradigm of preconceived beliefs into the meanings of words and scripture. We've learned how to do this from the deceived academic paradigm structure of schooled Jesuit-inspired education. But try looking through God's eyes or wisdom. Let's examine a binary structure of study in God's world.

I form the light, and create darkness:

I make peace, and create evil: I the Lord do all these things.

–Isaiah 45:7

God does good things, and Lucifer-Satan twists them into darkness and evil as deception. Therefore, we all function in a binary-effect world. We might make a wonderful dinner and have a sink full of dishes in dirty water. Build a beautiful home and have a dumpster full of waste material.

His word tells us there was light and peace before the darkness and evil, or the beginning. Therefore, Genesis 1:3 begins God's restoration of His kingdom, heaven, and earth with His light that the darkness waters were blocking. We will soon see the difference in the terms: created, form or make, and let.

Bible teachers have said we cannot understand the verse from Isaiah 45, but we can now if we grasp what we've learned about binary effects.

In God's world, there is eternal light; it became covered in darkness as deception. There was peace, and it became evil. He is giving us the afterthought because He formed the light to become His creations, and external darkness came upon His earth to destroy it all. Because there was peace, evil, as darkness raised its ugly face in the depths of eternity.

Solomon, arguably the wisest person who ever lived, immediately grasped the binary effects of God.

To every thing there is a season, and a time to every purpose under the heaven:

A time to be born, and a time to die; a time to plant, and a time to pluck up that which is planted;

A time to kill, and a time to heal; a time to break down, and a time to build up;

A time to weep, and a time to laugh; a time to mourn, and a time to dance;

A time to cast away stones, and a time to gather stones together; a time to embrace, and a time to refrain from embracing;

A time to get, and a time to lose; a time to keep, and a time to cast away;

A time to rend, and a time to sew; a time to keep silence, and a time to speak;

A time to love, and a time to hate; a time of war, and a time of peace.

–Ecclesiastes 3:1-8

If we are old enough, we've experienced these insights from Solomon, showing the binary effects of God. These verses show us what God worked through during the rebellion in His kingdom. During our lives, we experience what we encountered as spiritual beings on God's earth.

While as yet he had not made the earth, nor the fields, nor the highest part of the dust of the world.

When he established the clouds above: when he strengthened the fountains of the deep:

When he gave to the sea his decree, that the waters should not pass his commandment: when he appointed the foundations of the earth:

Then I was by him, as one brought up with him: and I was daily his delight, rejoicing always before him;

Rejoicing in the habitable part of his earth; and my delights were with the sons of men.

–Proverbs 8::26-31

These verses witness what we experienced from these events in our spirit bodies as sons of men.

The last verse, though, describes Eden, the better or more habitable part of the spiritual earth. We will see most of Adam's lineage, as spirit bodies, existed in Eden. However, we as spirit bodies existed on the rest of the spiritual earth's ground, or dust. More explanations will come later.

If we can change our physical views, the images we see daily are His binary effects to show us the history of His world.

If we've experienced any of these actions in Ecclesiastes, we have found the reactions from the spiritual actions of God, and there's no doubt about the existence of God anymore.

In The Beginning...
continued

These are the generations of the heavens and of the earth when they were created, in the day that the Lord God made the earth and the heavens,

–Genesis 2:4

We're going to skip down to chapter 2 for a moment. This is when the Lord God pre-made our universe-heaven and earth—in the spirit realm.

Look closely at what this scripture says:

"… heavens and earth when they were created, in the day…" (past tense)

"… that the Lord God made the earth and the heavens." It is the same time frame but a reaction-made, from the previous action-created. They are two separate events happening "in the Day."

Notice in the first sentence, heavens and earth flip to earth and heavens in the second part of the sentence.

Also, the word 'created' changes to 'made'.

And the obvious is the Lord God, translated as Yahweh Elohim, is an extended name from God or Elohim in the first chapter to when the Lord God made the earth and heavens.

The titles or names of the Lord God and God function as God, yet they are described separately from different perspectives.

How many times have people read this verse yet never seen the difference? Most Bible teachers skip over it.

The point is, while God was restoring His kingdom, heaven, and earth out of darkness, the Lord God was busy making our earth and heavens-universe from this same sea of darkness from Genesis 1, or "in the Day."

As previously stated, we've preconceived three words to mean the same in the creation story. They are: created, made, and let.

We will first look at created and made. These words are often interchanged, created, and made to mean the same thing. But they aren't in this verse, nor are they for us.

For example, we don't say, "I created breakfast this morning." We say, "I made breakfast this morning." Why do we say it this way?

Because the breakfast is a group of already-created ingredients (say eggs, bacon, and bread), and we will use those ingredients to make or cook our breakfast. We don't eat an egg still in its shell, take a bite out of a hog, or eat a lump of dough. We make something out of the already-created breakfast ingredients.

This is what the second part of the 2:4 verse says: the Lord God made the earth and heavens. It says it this way because it is from the created heavens and earth in Genesis 1:2. This spiritually 'made' earth and heavens will change to become our physical universe image.

In our Bible overview, we saw God often revealed His spirit realm to us, sometimes through what we might call miracles. We will continue to get a better understanding of the creation by looking into the spirit realm.

First, here is the old-school teaching.

The Creation—From Man

From the start, deceived religious teachers have told us Genesis 1 describes the creation of our universe-heaven, earth, space, and time—out of nothing.

Our earth is created without form and void, and darkness is upon the face of the deep. The Spirit of God moves above this darkness-deep-waters. It is supposedly the deepest part of our oceans, but they aren't "created" yet. The Bible trips up false doctrines.

As the deception continues, God creates everything else: light, an expanse or firmament, seas and land, grass, herbs, fruit-bearing trees, stars, the sun, moon, whales from the seas, fowl, land animals, and eventually, male-female man, all created within six days. This is the central deception taught to us throughout the ages.

We've falsely assumed God "created" all things here for our world, but the Genesis 1 chapter does not say created all things, which we will prove in just a moment.

Despite plants apparently growing and the male-female man already created in Genesis 1, Genesis 2 says the plants are not planted yet; animals and man are later formed—made from already created ingredients, not created.

Eve is separated from the man to form a woman. No one knows why God didn't do this in the first place in chapter 1. There is also no more mention of day or night, the stars, sun or moon, sea creatures, or fowl, which chapter 1 supposedly created.

Religious teachers explain that this is more detailed than in Chapter 1 and is occurring on our earth, but shown differently. We can see this is not true.

Eve eats from a tree that God told Adam not to eat from, or he will die. A talking serpent apparently governs this tree. First, Eve, then Adam, eat from the same tree, and they are cast out of the garden with the curse of death and difficulties in doing life. The garden is blocked entrance to the Tree of Life by cherubs and a flaming sword.

Adam 'knew' his wife Eve, and Cain, the first son from Eve, kills his brother Abel. We all know having children results from more than simply knowing someone, unless they are somewhere else.

Cain is ordered out of Eden. He moves east of Eden to a place called Nod and gets married. There is no teaching of where Nod came from or who Cain married; some say his sister, yet there is no mention of his sister.

We see Cain's descendants listed to the flood, and, unlike Adam's lineage, there is little mention of extended sons or daughters. For another unknown reason, 'knew' changes to 'begat'.

Later on, some relatives of God come to have sex with the beautiful women who existed on earth. They produced giants, and doing evil was the only thing on everyone's mind.

Thus, God gets ticked off and floods the earth to destroy almost everyone and everything to start over with a man named Noah, whom God had grace for, and his family. They were preserved from the flood in a huge boat called an ark, along with a pair of male and female animals and sevens of clean animals. The story doesn't say what made certain animals clean.

The rest of the story about the flood seems discombobulated or repeated because no one has shown us there are two renditions of the flood.

Despite non-eroded sediment layers worldwide to prove a global flood occurred on our earth, there doesn't appear to be any other physical evidence other than fossils buried deep in the earth.

We aren't arguing the details, just how, when, and where they occurred. Admittedly, this creation story sounds cryptic.

However, using the rest of the Bible and rational, constructive thinking, we should be able to figure out that none of these events occurred on our earth, and the flood started in God's world. We can fill in the blanks within Genesis 1:1–3, and where the creation story told to us has gaps.

There are other similar ancient creation tales as fantastic as this one, but we are to believe the religious teachers.

In summary, most religions teach God created everything in Genesis 1, and Chapter 2 gives more chronological detail after the creation in Genesis 1.

In the garden, there is a Tree of Life, a Tree of the Knowledge of Good and Evil, a talking serpent, cherubs, a flaming sword, and, later, sons of God having sex with women on the earth. Eventually, God cannot take it anymore and floods the earth.

No wonder any reasonably rational person who reads this would claim that if these things occurred on our current earth, they were vague science fiction or fables at best. Indeed, many fictional books do stem from this creation story, with a bit of a twist.

Can we rescue the story so it makes sense? Can we fill in the blanks?

We can, if we open ourselves to God's word and analyze the evidence, to comprehend the message behind the images from His world. We may still not believe the alternate creation story, but considering the context and other Bible verses, it should at least make sense with the rest of the Bible, teachers, atheist scientists, and our lives.

There isn't a preamble in the Bible that says we need to remove our common sense or not use the rational or constructive thinking God gave us before reading the Bible. There will be rationality in our discoveries if we can believe in God showing them in Genesis from His spirit world.

However, certain religions have had to make their listeners' minds ignorant to get us to believe what they've been taught, handed down through the centuries from religions, their doctrines, and hearsay.

Sometimes, an ounce of science or a bit of physics showed the religious teaching wrong. However, an additional ounce of spiritual teaching can prove the Bible correct.

Despite all this, the critical question is, why did the Lord God make a physical universe and earth for us? Perhaps eons of existence existed in God's kingdom when all was good. If all was well in His kingdom in the spirit realm, why did the Lord make a separate physical realm and earth for us?

We are told that when we die, those who have accepted Jesus as their savior will go back to God's kingdom. So, what are we doing here? Why are we here if the saved will return to heaven, where we started from? Why not just kick the evil beings out of His kingdom in the first place? Many people have devised theories about how our universe started, but no one has shown us why, until now.

Suppose we make one fundamental change in our thinking about the first seven chapters of Genesis. In that case, suddenly, it will all make sense, using our common sense, rational and constructive thinking—stepping out of the box from what we have learned from doctrinal religions. What is the alternative? What is the change?

We've arrogantly assumed, from our point of view, God is discussing our heaven, or universe, and our earth in Genesis 1. However, if we change our perspective to God's view, He isn't talking about our heaven and earth. He is showing us events in and on His heaven and earth! He temporarily lost His spiritual earth as dark waters.

We still have to know if there is a separate spirit realm with a heaven and earth, or God's kingdom, from our physical realm, or our universe and earth, our kingdom. Binary effect?

Perhaps we have to use our imagination until the Spirit of God reveals this Biblical alternate story into our spirit if we ask Him to do so.

The without form and void spiritual earth became our physical realm and our world in six days, either before or during a flood.

This is parallel to God restoring His kingdom in six days in His timeless eternity, out of the darkness-waters at the beginning of Genesis 1.

It is because Genesis 2 starts over with our historical creation story. God is showing us how we helped the fallen gods rebel and destroy His kingdom. We can find other Bible verses that fill in the background to tie the story together.

What caused God's earth to become without form and void in darkness's waters to become a flood? We joined the fallen gods in their rebellion against God—to their and our spiritual destruction.

Partial Background

It is doubtful the term day was a literal 'our world' day in God's world in Genesis 1 since the word 'day' is from the Hebrew word 'yom', which has a broad definition.

What we will plainly show are six events restored as days of God extracting what He wanted out of the dark waters and back into His light. Isn't that what the day does for us? Brings our earth stuff out of darkness into the light of day again? Images from God in Genesis 1!

The first chapter describes six restorative events, called days, of God bringing his original creation out of darkness into His light of eternal day again.

The physical realm doesn't become our reality until chapter 7, or after the dark waters of the flood are formed.

It becomes much easier to understand our current universe and earth's formation, which scientifically appears to be billions of years old, when we realize it was pre-made somewhere else, with live spiritual beings already in existence.

Perhaps it took eons of destruction from the rebellious events on God's earth or kingdom to produce the darkness-waters that the Lord God divides out to become our universal physical realm. It perhaps took ages for Lucifer, his followers, and our spirit bodies to destroy most of God's earth.

It will not take eons to destroy our earth and universe again. It will happen in an instant. Don't let the binary effects escape our reading.

The destructed part is where God tossed everything out of His kingdom—Lucifer, fallen gods, and, later, our spirits—into a sea of darkness.

Out of this fallen darkness, God first restored His light: heaven, land, seas, plants, trees, luminaries like stars, a greater and lesser light, created new enormous sea creatures, restored land animals, and male-female man created in God's image. After He finished, the remnant of the darkened universal sea became our physical realm.

This is how God restored His spiritual earth, and the Lord God formed our physical realm universe. God already spiritually created everything from the beginning of the story, and the Lord God made our universe from God's destroyed earth. It was the remnant "without form and void" spiritual earth.

The thing that hath been, it is that which shall be; and that which is done is that which shall be done: and there is no new thing under the sun.

Is there any thing whereof it may be said, See, this is new? it hath been already of old time, which was before us.

–Ecclesiastes 1:9-10

Solomon gets the alternate creation story. We are replaying our spiritual lives on our earth, showing us why we are here. What we will discover is Eden was never on our planet, except for when it was temporarily flushed in the flood into a separated section of hell called Abraham's Bosom. This is where the OT people of faith went when they died before Jesus' resurrection from the dead.

"Dust," from the ground of this spiritual, fallen earth, is where the Lord formed man as an eternal, living soul. His soul existed within a spiritual body called flesh. The Lord God had formed man to work with God to restore His kingdom, which the fallen gods destroyed.

This is probably starting an earthquake in our foundation of traditional learning, handed down through the centuries. It may even sound more disturbing than the conventional story. A few of the readers are probably shaking their heads.

Please allow God to remove our deception, or at least show His version of the creation story in our minds and hearts. This book takes nothing away from God's eternal plan of salvation through the shed blood of our Savior on the cross and His resurrection, which is the most important part of the Bible. It enhances our understanding of why Jesus had to come to our earth to save us.

It also shows where our eternal home will be if we accept His plan for saving us from ourselves and what we will do when we get there.

But why did the Lord God make our universe and earth? If He already had a home for us in His spirit kingdom, why did we end up outside in our physical realm?

Because we were rebelliously bad—joining the false gods and fully intending to destroy God's kingdom through our rebellion against Him.

The Lord God gave us a time-out.

Genesis 1-Regenerated

We saw how Genesis readers skipped understanding three words, thinking they meant the same thing. We've seen two of these words already: created and made. Formed and made are essentially the same, which modifies something already created. However, there is a third word used in Genesis—let.

It isn't our fault though, not seeing the difference in translation, as Bible scholars and teachers purposely changed the written word and allowed these 'made' words to be changed to created in their teachings. It is obvious, God wanted to use the 'made' words from created for a purpose.

Created, made, and let are used separately in Genesis 1. Usually, we should use the word made or formed to refer to something already created. However, 'let' is used differently, as if something is blocked.

We might say, "Let the dog out," because the door is an obstacle, blocking the dog from getting out. Thus, when God says, "Let," He is dividing or removing the obstacle, telling the darkness-waters to let out what He wants to begin His eternal restoration project.

In Genesis 1, the term created is only used three times—in the beginning of His heaven and earth, the enormous new sea creatures, and with the newly restored male-female man.

Let is used when the darkness-waters were the obstacle blocking something already created from getting out into the light of Day again in God's kingdom.

After the eternal darkness, or the deep, diffused into waters and later became a flood, we will see in verse 3 that God has released His light into His kingdom again.

Simultaneously, the Lord God is making what will become our universe in darkness, which God is now dividing out, revealing more of His binary effects.

And God said, Let there be light: and there was light.

And God saw the light, that it was good: and God divided the light from the darkness.

And God called the light Day, and the darkness he called Night. And the evening and the morning were the first day.

–Genesis 1:3-5

We can plainly see, God has let the light out from the dark waters, and it was still working as He says, "… that it was good." The light was not created because it always existed. Remember in Isaiah 45:7, "I form the light, and create darkness." As the light originally emanated from God, He formed creation.

It appears from these verses, God sees His kingdom as Day, and our physical realm as Night.

What Lucifer didn't realize was when he turned against God, his light would go out. Lucifer caused the darkness with his fallen beings, who rebelled against God. It was a natural event, as there is darkness when we turn off the light.

And from the wicked their light is withholden, and the high arm shall be broken.

–Job 38:12-15

God has opened the door in the darkness-waters to let the light out, and now His eternal light is restored forever in His kingdom.

Verse 5 says, "And the evening and the morning were the first day." If this were the creation of our universe and earth, which it isn't, the verse would have said, "And the evening, and the Night, and the morning were the first day."

It doesn't say 'night' because there is no night in God's kingdom, which is why it isn't mentioned. Neither is there any sun or moon. His light is everywhere.

And there shall be no night there; and they need no candle, neither light of the sun;

for the Lord God giveth them light: and they shall reign for ever.

–Revelation 22:5

All of His restored creations will radiate light once again. The days mentioned after this Genesis verse do not mention the night from evening to morning. It has been divided out forever into the night of making our universe.

To restore God's earth, He uses something called a firmament. God had uncovered part of the deep darkness-waters, letting the darkened images out into the light again.

This might be like us, as if we are using a tool, letting our images of onions or carrots out of our darkened earth garden, bringing them into the light of day, and washing the dark dirt off our veggies. This is how He restores His kingdom, using a firmament tool to bring the light of everything back into His earth.

And God said, Let there be a firmament in the midst of the waters, and let it divide the waters from the waters.

And God made the firmament, and divided the waters which were under the firmament from the waters which were above the firmament: and it was so.

And God called the firmament Heaven. And the evening and the morning were the second day.

–Genesis 1:6-8

Some of the newer Bibles translate the firmament as a vault and heaven as the sky. These versions are, allegedly, the poorest Bible translations ever written. However, various religious teachers use these Bibles, which block the Genesis creation story, among other spiritual revelations.

The reason argued as the lowest translations is they are more of a negotiation among religious leaders than an accurate translation and perhaps fulfill their doctrinal agendas. The translators also took the lesser meanings of translation in order to sell a different Bible version.

The first and primary Hebrew definition of a firmament is an expanse or a firm expanse, not a vault. It translates as heaven, not sky. The expanse and heaven words are in context; the vault and sky are not. Regardless, these verses are rich in His binary effects. The waters above the firmament form His restored heaven and earth. The dark waters below will form our universe.

God had divided the darkness to reveal His spiritual light, and now He is dividing the waters from the waters with a firmament to show the rest of His restoration.

Some Bible scholars believe there was a circle of water above our atmosphere at one time, and this verse states this firmament divides those waters from the waters on earth.

For this they willingly are ignorant of, that by the word of God the heavens were of old, and the earth standing out of the water and in the water:

–2nd Peter 3:5

Even if it were the case here, it isn't because this verse is Peter describing the pre-destructed earth when "the heavens were of old" and the earth destructing into something without form and void. We are now seeing the restoring firmament as a force, dividing, or sifting device.

This firmament sifts through the darkness and extracts what God needs to restore the foundation of His kingdom. When it finished its job, it became a foundation in heaven.

And above the firmament that was over their heads was the likeness of a throne, as the appearance of a sapphire stone: and upon the likeness of the throne was the likeness as the appearance of a man above upon it.

–Ezekiel 1:26

Ezekiel saw the firmament when God opened heaven for him to view. Waters is also often a symbol of people and nations.

And he saith unto me, The waters which thou sawest, where the whore sitteth, are peoples, and multitudes, and nations, and tongues.

–Revelation 17:15

Later, we will see the flood occur after God restored His earth. The firmament will play a role in separating the righteous beings from the fallen ones during the flood.

To look deeper into this image, we can understand the darkness waters came because of the fallen gods and man. The spirits of the fallen will get flushed under the depths of the seas or the midst of our earth to be physically born later.

The other righteous or chosen spirits who called upon the name of the Lord will be restored during the flood. Although their spirits came to our earth to be born, the Lord also restored these saved in our earth to God's heaven and earth after Jesus' resurrection.

The fallen spirit beings, angels and us, were flushed out of the spirit realm into our earth, and some cried out to God to save us. This is how God foreknew whom Jesus would save as the firstborn, after Jesus.

For whom he did foreknow, he also did predestinate to be conformed to the image of his Son, that he might be the firstborn among many brethren.

Moreover whom he did predestinate, them he also called: and whom he called, them he also justified: and whom he justified, them he also glorified.

–Romans 8:29-30

Who hath saved us, and called us with an holy calling, not according to our works, but according to his own purpose and grace, which was given us in Christ Jesus before the world began

–2nd Timothy 1:9

It doesn't mean that if we didn't cry out to God before our world began—to rescue us during the flood—He couldn't restore us because He can if we cry out to God to save us during our lives.

This is the mystery of God: who first saved the Jews who accepted Yeshua as their savior and then the non-Jews as Gentiles.

Whereby, when ye read, ye may understand my knowledge in the mystery of Christ

Which in other ages was not made known unto the sons of men, as it is now revealed unto his holy apostles and prophets by the Spirit;

That the Gentiles should be fellowheirs, and of the same body, and partakers of his promise in Christ by the gospel:

–Ephesians 3:4-6

We are fellow heirs with the Jewish people who accept Yeshua or Jesus as their Messiah or Savior. There will be more clarity when God first restores Adam and his descendants into the light.

After God started the restoration, the Hebrew scholars believed this firmament now signified the land holding back the seas in heaven. The firmament boundary separating heaven and our realm may prevent us from seeing into the spirit world unless God permits us.

Restoring His Earth

And God said, Let the waters under the heaven be gathered together unto one place, and let the dry land appear: and it was so.

And God called the dry land Earth; and the gathering together of the waters called he Seas: and God saw that it was good.

–Genesis 1:9-10

Our old academic paradigm of preconceived thought has taught us that God is creating our land and seas, but again, it doesn't say create; it says "let."

This is the firmament restoring a portion of seas and land. He is moving the waters aside first so the land can appear. After, He takes a portion of the waters that he moved and restores them as land and seas. They will expand forever.

As the firmament expands now with His restored earth, it also stretches the land and seas. His restored earth with the seas will appear and look like our earth, except on a much grander scale from the expanse of the firmament.

The firmament first brought a portion of the land to appear from the darkened waters, and He also restored a portion of the waters into seas. The rest of the waters below the firmament will become a flood to and as our universe.

And God said, Let the earth bring forth grass, the herb yielding seed, and the fruit tree yielding fruit after his kind, whose seed is in itself, upon the earth: and it was so.

And the earth brought forth grass, and herb yielding seed after his kind, and the tree yielding fruit, whose seed was in itself, after his kind: and God saw that it was good.

–Genesis 1:11-12

After His light restored plants and trees, they started growing again. People have often asked, "Why did God create these things before the sun?" Now we know these aren't plants or trees on our earth; they are in God's light and will emit light. They don't need a sun.

This is the formation of the Garden of Eden. When we want to landscape our yards, we go to the garden center and a nursery to get plants and trees. The garden is the starting nursery for God's earth. It plays a major role in the restoration, along with animals and Adam and Eve.

God is commanding the darkness to let His light-formed original creations return to spiritual existence, or light again.

And God said, Let there be lights in the firmament of the heaven to divide the day from the night; and let them be for signs, and for seasons, and for days, and years:

And let them be for lights in the firmament of the heaven to give light upon the earth: and it was so.

And God made two great lights; the greater light to rule the day, and the lesser light to rule the night: he made the stars also.

And God set them in the firmament of the heaven to give light upon the earth,

And to rule over the day and over the night, and to divide the light from the darkness: and God saw that it was good.

–Genesis 1:14-18

These verses are an extension or completion of the previous Genesis 1:3-6 verses, where God released the light back into His world and forever divided the darkness into night.

If this was our earth and the heaven translation was sky, these verses would say the lights were set in our sky, which is absurd.

There is never a mention of our earth rotating to allow day and night. In addition, the night is no longer there, as it is controlled outside or divided out of His kingdom. However, what is the purpose of the restored lights?

Imagine ourselves standing in heaven, with lights emanating from everywhere, revealing the days and years of everything that has happened or will happen.

Lights are also translated as luminaries or light-bearers. Lucifer was apparently the greatest light-bearer other than God. Lucifer fell with at least a third (trillions) of the angels, who were all radiating light. God makes new luminaries.

These spiritual lights may reveal the knowledge of God throughout eternity. They will never again allow the darkness of deception to come into God's kingdom.

As we restore His kingdom, they will become new days, and many restored days will be called years. There will still be seasons on God's earth, but we won't have to wait for them now. We can choose to go to the different seasons on His earth.

The two greater and lesser lights are not the sun and moon. If they were, the Bible would have said as such. We already know there isn't a need for a sun or moon. These lights describe the day and evening, or a greater and lesser light.

These lights will no longer permit access to the darkness or darkness to light. Perhaps they are controlled and ruled over by Michael and Gabriel. They will forever "divide the light from the darkness."

And God said, Let the waters bring forth abundantly the moving creature that hath life, and fowl that may fly above the earth in the open firmament of heaven.

And God created great whales, and every living creature that moveth, which the waters brought forth abundantly, after their kind, and every winged fowl after his kind: and God saw that it was good.

And God blessed them, saying, Be fruitful, and multiply, and fill the waters in the seas, and let fowl multiply in the earth.

–Genesis 1:20-22

The first thing God said was to let the waters bring forth lots of moving creatures that have life and the fowl. It doesn't say they were created in the seas—they already had life in the waters. This means they were already created with life.

It then follows the fowl released are going to fly around in heaven while they multiply in the earth. Again, it doesn't say our sky.

However, next it says, God created great whales when they came from the waters with the living creatures. It doesn't say the whales came from the seas, but came from the waters to fill the waters in the seas.

"After their kind", means they were already in existence and can reproduce more of their kind, and God is letting them restore to life.

The KJV Bible translated the verse as "great whales", but the translation means enormous sea monsters, dragons, or serpents. These are new sea animals that can rise from the sea to fly around in heaven. They can exist in the waters, on land, or fly in heaven.

The Book of Job, chapters 40 and 41, describe monstrous creatures and speak of behemoths or dragons on the earth, and fire sneezing Leviathans from the sea. These two Job chapters may describe these "whales" from Genesis, which may be more like working pets to us.

And God said, Let the earth bring forth the living creature after his kind, cattle, and creeping thing, and beast of the earth after his kind: and it was so.

And God made the beast of the earth after his kind, and cattle after their kind, and every thing that creepeth upon the earth after his kind: and God saw that it was good.

–Genesis 1:24.25

There is no creation here either. It is obvious the earth held the land animals, and God told the land to let or release them. These land animals came from the garden in Eden, or, judging by the trillions of animals we have slaughtered, no shortage of restored land animals will exist. God makes or restores them, with changes made to function in the restored world.

Just as the great sea monsters will be in charge of restoring sea life, the beasts will restore land animals, all after their kind.

On the new earth, animals will be helpers to assist the saved in restoring the kingdom. They will be like our pets.

The wolf also shall dwell with the lamb, and the leopard shall lie down with the kid; and the calf and the young lion and the fatling together; and a little child shall lead them.

And the cow and the bear shall feed; their young ones shall lie down together: and the lion shall eat straw like the ox.

–Isaiah 11:6-7

We've seen many animals, if raised together from birth, who might otherwise be predators and prey, grow, play, and live together without harming each other. Images from heaven!

Restored Man

And God said, Let us make man in our image, after our likeness: and let them have dominion over the fish of the sea, and over the fowl of the air, and over the cattle, and over all the earth, and over every creeping thing that creepeth upon the earth.

So God created man in his own image, in the image of God created he him; male and female created he them.

And God blessed them, and God said unto them, Be fruitful, and multiply, and replenish the earth, and subdue it: and have dominion over the fish of the sea, and over the fowl of the air, and over every living thing that moveth upon the earth.

–Genesis 1:26-28

The first verse says, "Let us make man...". Hopefully, by now, we know 'let' means removing the obstacle, and he is about to be made or created as a new man in God's restored earth.

There was already man, either buried in the earth's dust or existing in Eden. We will see Adam and his lineage, other than Cain, will be the first to have God make them and be created in His image and likeness.

These paragraphs from Genesis find our three favorite words: Let, Make, and Created.

First, God says, "Let us..." He is confirming with the Godhead to opening the door for our resurrection to occur in God's "... image, after our likeness," to create man as restored.

We will see when the Lord God made man; He formed him from the dust of the destructed earth. This certainly was not in the image and likeness of God.

If Adam and Eve had eaten from the Tree of Life, God's image and likeness would have been created into their spirit, and we wouldn't be here, quarantined on our earth.

God created a resurrected man, as male-female, to restore originally what man could have had through Adam. This restored man will be recombined with the female and have just one name. And we will once again have dominion over all animals.

We don't currently have dominion over the fish of the sea or the fowl of the air. They do whatever they want to do. We are horrible managers of our earth, resources, and animals.

Our resurrection from calling on the name of the Lord is the only time Jesus restores us in His image through our salvation. We will maintain His likeness, doing the things Jesus did. We will have His authority over all of His kingdom to continue making all things new again through replenishing His earth.

We were initially supposed to be building His kingdom world. Instead, we joined Lucifer with the fallen angels and destroyed most of His original creation.

Since God uses the words "Let us" in the verse, something had stopped God from restoring us, like the door blocking the dog from getting outside—it was our sins and rebellion.

"Make man." the Lord already formed a man who disobeyed God, but now he is changed. "Created in our image and likeness." God created the male-female to receive God's image and likeness through the eternal plan of salvation through Jesus.

If we accept this plan, we will receive His attributes, righteousness, and holiness to carry out His will in His kingdom.

The Psalmist, David, gave us images of our falling away and restoration in Psalms when his soul cried out to God to save him during the flood.

In the following verses, David witnesses the experience of his soul and spirit during God's transformation of the destroyed earth into our universe and his resurrection into God's kingdom. It gives us great insight into what we now know about where our universe came from.

Notice, the first thing David does is call upon the Lord, and by doing so, he will be saved. He shares his experience from the destructed earth.

I will call upon the Lord, who is worthy to be praised: so shall I be saved from mine enemies.

The sorrows of death compassed me, and the floods of ungodly men made me afraid.

The sorrows of hell compassed me about: the snares of death prevented me.

In my distress I called upon the Lord, and cried unto my God: he heard my voice out of his temple, and my cry came before him, even into his ears.

Then the earth shook and trembled; the foundations also of the hills moved and were shaken, because he was wroth.

There went up a smoke out of his nostrils, and fire out of his mouth devoured: coals were kindled by it.

He bowed the heavens also, and came down: and darkness was under his feet.

And he rode upon a cherub, and did fly: yea, he did fly upon the wings of the wind.

He made darkness his secret place; his pavilion round about him were dark waters and thick clouds of the skies.

At the brightness that was before him his thick clouds passed, hail stones and coals of fire.

The Lord also thundered in the heavens, and the Highest gave his voice; hail stones and coals of fire.

Yea, he sent out his arrows, and scattered them; and he shot out lightnings, and discomfited them.

Then the channels of waters were seen, and the foundations of the world were discovered at thy rebuke, O Lord, at the blast of the breath of thy nostrils.

He sent from above, he took me, he drew me out of many waters.

He delivered me from my strong enemy, and from them which hated me: for they were too strong for me.

They prevented me in the day of my calamity: but the Lord was my stay.

He brought me forth also into a large place; he delivered me, because he delighted in me.

The Lord rewarded me according to my righteousness; according to the cleanness of my hands hath he recompensed me.

–Psalm 18:3-20

Most Bible teachers claim this is just Jewish poetic prose, but poetic of what? They haven't seen the spiritual images.

Obviously, these things never occurred on our planet. We can now understand these events happened on God's dark waters of a without form and void earth as they transferred into making our universe through a flood.

It is apparent, the hail stones and coals of fire from His destructed earth produced the asteroids and comets in our universe.

Other verses from the Psalms describe the same, but this is the most interesting evidence of what has been shown so far concerning the destruction of God's earth through a flood into our earth and bringing in the righteous through the dividing firmament, which is now called heaven.

We will spend eternity rebuilding what we almost destroyed. There is no rush, though; we have all of eternity. The saved will be created in His image and likeness to accomplish His will.

And God said, Behold, I have given you every herb bearing seed, which is upon the face of all the earth, and every tree, in the which is the fruit of a tree yielding seed; to you it shall be for meat.

And to every beast of the earth, and to every fowl of the air, and to every thing that creepeth upon the earth, wherein there is life, I have given every green herb for meat: and it was so.

And God saw every thing that he had made, and, behold, it was very good. And the evening and the morning were the sixth day.

–Genesis 1:29-31

There will be food for us, and for the animals everywhere we go. It is difficult to imagine all the blessings we will have on the restored earth. We could picnic on a tropical island and get there on the back of a Leviathan.

On the beach, a group of monkeys or gorillas may bring us bananas and a bunch of grapes of every color and taste. Maybe a train of wandering land animals will come and sing to us in perfect harmony and join us in our feast. Perhaps a dragon sneezes a fire for us so we can roast marshmallows.

These are just some of the mind-blowing wonders that may await the repentant, spirit-born disciples of Jesus. We can use our greatest imaginations and can't even think of how incredible our restored life will be forever.

And what about our job when we aren't relaxing on our new earth?

And they shall build the old wastes, they shall raise up the former desolations, and they shall repair the waste cities, the desolations of many generations.

–Isaiah 61:4

Scholars will argue that this is the prophecy of the 1948 restoration of Israel. But as we have seen, there are also spiritual images within Bible verses referring to His kingdom.

Our permanent job will be to restore His kingdom that the false gods and our spirit bodies destroyed.

There will be food we never knew existed, and of never-ending supply. Eating will be a blessing for us, not a necessity.

And God blessed the seventh day, and sanctified it: because that in it he had rested from all his work which God created and made.

–Genesis 2:3

Here we see the difference again between created and made. All is very good again in God's kingdom, which He both originally created and later restored or made. Everything the firmament extracted from the darkness waters or the flood was restored and made new again.

Thus, Genesis 1 summarizes God restoring His earth and heaven. In a moment, we start over again in Chapter 2, discovering why God's earth became the darkness on the deep.

First, 'let us' discover the obstacles of religion.

Religions as Obstacles to God

"You have to know the past to understand the present."

– Carl Sagan

Some people don't like to learn history. Unfortunately, they don't realize that history often reveals our deceptions. We can get drawn into errors established as religious orthodoxy and in politics, science, education, and other institutions. If we studied history, we would not be bamboozled or so quickly felled as prey.

Before we continue, we should see how religions have set obstacles in our way to prevent us from becoming loyal disciples of Jesus. We need to look into the dark waters of the past and extract the truth of salvation, which religions have buried.

In order to discover when religious-type worship started, we have to look back in the OT to find a man named Nimrod. He was the first person on our earth to be led astray by the fallen false gods, who were flushed into our earth during the flood. Nimrod enslaved children and killed animals after the flood to defy and rebel against God.

And Cush begat Nimrod: he began to be a mighty one in the earth.

He was a mighty hunter before the LORD: wherefore it is said, Even as Nimrod the mighty hunter before the LORD.

And the beginning of his kingdom was Babel, and Erech, and Accad, and Calneh, in the land of Shinar.

–Genesis 10:8-10

The false gods, and now Lucifer as Satan, determined they were going to steal their way back into the kingdom of God by building a tower that would penetrate the sky, and therefore presumably gain access again into the spiritual kingdom.

For thou hast said in thine heart, I will ascend into heaven, I will exalt my throne above the stars of God:

I will sit also upon the mount of the congregation, in the sides of the north:

–Isaiah 14:13

And the angels which kept not their first estate, but left their own habitation, he hath reserved in everlasting chains under darkness unto the judgment of the great day.

–Jude 1:6

The fallen beings did not know how far they fell or where they were in their darkness. These demons of false gods deceived Nimrod to build a tower by enslaving the children to work in tar, or slime pits, so the fallen beings with Satan could ascend back into heaven.

And they said one to another, Go to, let us make brick, and burn them thoroughly. And they had brick for stone, and slime had they for morter.

And they said, Go to, let us build us a city and a tower, whose top may reach unto heaven; and let us make us a name, lest we be scattered abroad upon the face of the whole earth.

And the LORD came down to see the city and the tower, which the children of men builded.

–Genesis 11:3-5

We know this tower to be Babel, in that God caused all the builders to speak in languages no one knew, and therefore they quit building. Others built a city around the tower as the first pagan temple and continued to build more cities, with more temples until today.

After a kingdom conquered another kingdom, they adopted their gods as their own and changed their names. Later, the people in Samaria began worshiping these idols along with the Jewish God (2 Kings:17).

It continued into the time of Jesus, when the Jewish leadership would worship the Roman gods, stemming from Babylon, along with the temple and sacrifices for Yah, or Yahweh, the Jewish God.[3]

When Jesus came to our earth, He didn't chastise the IRS of the day or the tax collectors. He didn't even condemn the Romans for all the Jews' suffering when the Romans daily whipped or crucified many of His fellow Jews.

Instead, He took to task the Jewish religious leaders, who were spewing their religious deception out of the temple, placing obstacles between people and God. In His eyes, they were the most evil.

Jesus exposed the temple leadership to what they were doing in their mixed religion. The apostle John would later call this type of blended worship, Mystery Babylon.

But woe unto you, scribes and Pharisees, hypocrites! for ye shut up the kingdom of heaven against men: for ye neither go in yourselves, neither suffer ye them that are entering to go in.

Woe unto you, scribes and Pharisees, hypocrites! for ye devour widows' houses, and for a pretence make long prayer: therefore ye shall receive the greater damnation.

Woe unto you, scribes and Pharisees, hypocrites! for ye compass sea and land to make one proselyte, and when he is made, ye make him twofold more the child of hell than yourselves.

–Matthew 23:13-15

---

[3] Most readers will recognize the current mistranslated name of God as Jehovah; religions changed it from Yah during the middle ages. Jehovah is not found in the Orthodox Jewish Bible.

One wonders if Jesus would say the same to the religious leaders today?

After Jesus resurrected from the dead, He started His true church at Pentecost, signified by His followers internally receiving the fire of His Spirit to rekindle our spirit into the kingdom of God.

Lucifer, now Satan, failed to stop the lineage from Adam to Jesus and keep a person from gaining back their citizenship in the kingdom of God. All the devil could do now is deceive the world into not using the tools to receive our salvation. He put together religious deception as an avenue to bypass the direct plan of God to restore us.

For such are false apostles, deceitful workers, transforming themselves into the apostles of Christ. And no marvel; for Satan himself is transformed into an angel of light. Therefore, it is no great thing if his ministers also be transformed as the ministers of righteousness; whose end shall be according to their works.

–2 Corinthians 11:13-15

In his travels, Paul discovered false teachers were claiming to be apostles of a type of religion, trying to seduce his followers away from the true Gospel or salvation from God. One of these groups became known as the Gnostic.

There were branches of the Gnostic religion that eventually infiltrated other religions. In Jerusalem, the temple leadership was trying to get the converted Jews from Peter and other apostles to renounce Jesus and take on their Judaism laws again as their salvation. Many probably chose this route to avoid the horrific persecution of the Jewish leadership.

In any case, various sects were popping up to remove the grace of God and, instead, promote a 'works' ethic, primarily to acquire divine knowledge beyond the salvation of Jesus.

This would eventually form the basis of the Roman Universal Religion with their ecumenical, or joining together, councils where many sects, some from the generic Gnostic belief systems, would be combined into one united religion, or Catholic.

All 'Christian' religions today, either directly or indirectly, branch off of the original Roman religion. Many non-denominational churches have started in the past century, some of which have discovered deceptive religious doctrines, while others have become evangelists to enrich themselves. Jesus' true church has been handed down to us through His Spirit baptism. It bypasses religions of any sort.

His fire-baptized church has survived centuries of persecution despite the devil, through religions and others, trying to slaughter it out of existence.

If a person did a basic search (Flowchart of Christian Denominations) on where their denomination came from, they would find it links back in history to the Roman religion.

Most of the time, a denomination is divided or splits off because of differences in opinions on how religious rites and their beliefs or doctrines should be practiced.

These disagreements turned into each religion, believing theirs was the only true one, ignoring the church Jesus started at Pentecost. It has bloomed into more than 30,000 different denominations today.

In the 19th century, a few religions promoted a particular belief about the coming of Jesus or why He hadn't returned yet. They began publishing tracts or articles to develop their specific false doctrines outside of the Bible.[4]

They didn't believe in Jesus as God, saying no one would know when the end would come. They ignore the steps of salvation as the sole avenue to eternal life, and instead, they produce additional publications on why they believe their religion is more accurate through their false doctrines.

Knowing these things from history, we can be set free from religions and their self-promoted doctrines. The only way back to God's kingdom is to get in contact with Jesus.

---

[4]See: Millerites, Adventists, Watchtower Bible and Tract Society, and Christian Scientists

Jesus saith unto him, I am the way, the truth, and the life: no man cometh unto the Father, but by me.

–John 14:6

I tell you, Nay: but, except yet ye repent, ye shall all likewise perish.

–Luke 13:3

Jesus answered and said unto him, Verily, verily, I say unto thee, Except a man be born again, he cannot see the kingdom of God.

–John 3:3

I indeed baptize you with water unto repentance, but he that cometh after me is mightier than I, whose shoes I am not worthy to bear: he shall baptize you with the Holy Ghost, <u>and with fire</u>: (From John the Baptist, underline added)

–Matthew 3:11

Then said Jesus unto his disciples, If any man will come after me, let him deny himself, and take up his cross, and follow me.

–Matthew 16:24

But the Comforter, which is the Holy Ghost, whom the Father will send in my name, he shall teach you all things, and bring all things to your remembrance, whatsoever I have said unto you.

–John 14:26

It is doubtful that many people have seen or heard God's eternal plan of salvation in this order. Repent, be born again with His baptism of fire, follow Jesus, and His Spirit will teach us all things. They are the keys to His kingdom. After we do these things; He personally makes us His disciples.

When we are His disciples, we will do the same things Jesus did, and we will receive His different spiritual gifts.

For to one is given by the Spirit the word of wisdom; to another the word of knowledge by the same Spirit;

To another faith by the same Spirit; to another the gifts of healing by the same Spirit;

To another the working of miracles; to another prophecy; to another discerning of spirits; to another divers kinds of tongues; to another the interpretation of tongues:

But all these worketh that one and the selfsame Spirit, dividing to every man severally as he will.

–1 Corinthians 12:8-11

This is genuine Christianity, which is not passed down through religions because only Jesus can personally make us His disciples through the fire baptism of His Spirit, and give us His spiritual gifts.

Overall, we are saved through God's grace and faith in the blood sacrifice of Jesus at Calvary, not through membership in any religion.

Words can only lead us to the Tree of Life. It is up to each person individually to seek God, repent, ask to become born again in His Spirit, listen, and follow His teachings.

When His Spirit blesses you with His gift(s), you will know beyond all doubt that God has resurrected your soul into His kingdom.

When The Lord God Made Our Earth

This next section is an overview into the "creation", providing more detail when appropriate. God has restored His kingdom's light, so the eternal restoration of His earth can go on forever. It is also known as Mount Zion.

But ye are come unto mount Sion, and unto the city of the living God, the heavenly Jerusalem, and to an innumerable company of angels,

–Hebrews 12:22

It perhaps isn't an actual mountain but more of a separate dimension or destination, i.e., heaven. We see there was/is His city named Jerusalem, as on our earth. Adam and Eve were to be the first in the continuance of restoring God's earth, and we were to follow. The Lord's earth was separated from this restoration.

We saw how Genesis chapter 1 is a summary statement of God restoring His kingdom after it was almost destroyed. When God lifted the firmament out of the darkness-waters, everything He needed came into His earth with each event or day.

While God restored His earth, the rest of the darkness-waters— were left for the Lord God to form what would become our physical realm universe-heavens and earth.

In the next Genesis chapter, 2, beginning with verse 4, we saw the Lord God making what would become our earth and heavens.

From Genesis chapters 2–6, we will learn why we fell into a complete darkness of rebellion and destruction, causing the restoring events of His kingdom in Genesis chapter 1.

This world of darkness, rebellion, and destruction becomes our universe and earth-physical realm through a flood.

Scientists realize everything needs a cause and effect, and this is it concerning the formation of our physical realm.

The act of God flushing, described as a flood, the darkness and rebellion as a sea out of His spiritual kingdom, includes "in the Day", restoring His earth and universe, or heaven.

Scientists have discovered trillions of enormous volumes of water in our universe, and many planets and moons are made of ice, remnants from the sea of darkened waters, and flood from God's world.[5]

During the flood, we will discover there were two arks and floods, or at least one ark and flood accomplishing two things. God conducts the first spiritual flood. Out of this flood of darkness, is when God used the firmament to restore His kingdom.

The remnant flood from the Lord, lasting for over a year, formed our current universe and earth.

At the start of the spiritual flood is when God begins the Genesis 1 story, "In the beginning," and the flood culminates with Noah releasing the Spirit of God from the ark, symbolized as a dove, where it reflects in Genesis 1:3, "And the spirit moved upon the face of the earth."

---

[5] **Dyches, Preston; Chou, Felcia (7 April 2015). . NASA. Archived from THE ORIGINAL on 10 April 2015. "THE SOLAR SYSTEM AND BEYOND IS AWASH IN WATER"**

Thus, when the Lord formed our earth and heavens, the Garden of Eden wasn't upon our physical earth, and neither were Adam nor any of his spiritual descendants up to Noah and his family.

They all existed in God's spiritual earth during Lucifer's rebellion, and so did our spirit bodies, arguably from Cain's descendants.

Adam's descendants were restored into heaven before the flood, and only Cain's descendants, as our spirits and fallen gods, were in the flood of our universe and earth.

The flood moved our souls and Eden into our earth, where we would be physically born, and until Jesus' resurrection, where we would remain. Before His resurrection, the righteous went to a place called Paradise, or Abraham's Bosom, which was Eden, located somewhere in our earth, possibly below the oceans.

The evidence of these events will be shown when we get into the later chapters.

We can know these creation events didn't occur on our earth because we will see a talking serpent, cherubs, a flaming sword, and the Lord God originally walking and talking with Adam. These were all spiritual realm events.

We didn't and don't have these things happening on our physical earth. Until Jesus arrived, communication between God and people was usually performed by angels as messengers of God. After Pentecost, this spiritual communication occurs from the Spirit of God through our souls as fire-baptized, born-again believers.

We can also know, Genesis 1 is the restoration of His heaven and earth because, in the Book of Revelation, John sees a new heaven and earth in the spiritual realm.

And I saw a new heaven and a new earth: for the first heaven and the first earth were passed away; and there was no more sea.

–Revelation 21:1

Since John is viewing the spirit realm in Revelation, he sees God's first heaven and earth have passed away, as have the sea since it became our darkened universe, which will eventually dissolve into almost complete darkness. It seems this is what scientists call–dark energy.

This verse, Rev. 21:1, is so far confirming what we have read concerning Genesis 1.

For the most part, in our history, all the Gentile teachers of the Bible have learned the scriptures filtered through false doctrines, primarily from the false church or Roman religion.

This Roman religion, with St. Ignatius, started the militant Jesuit Priests, or Society of Jesus, from the Council of Trent to counter Protestants who were attacking Roman religious doctrines.

The society infiltrated seminaries, universities, and instituted Catholic schools to lead people astray with the Roman religious doctrines, including the doctrine of the end-times. This religion stems from the revised Roman Empire, or Holy Roman Empire, which started around the eighth century AD.

However, probably the major argument is this raises another issue. If our earth and universe came during the flood, and according to Jewish genealogy, this means our earth-universe didn't come into physical existence until about 2450 BC, our time. And by scientific reckoning, this is arguably impossible. Or is it?

We don't know for sure how long people existed in the spiritual realm, as perhaps years were ages or such.

But, beloved, be not ignorant of this one thing, that one day is with the Lord as a thousand years, and a thousand years as one day.

–2 Peter 3:8

These time measurements are not literal because a thousand is symbolic of infinite or not exact.

For every beast of the forest is mine, and the cattle upon a thousand hills.

–Psalm 50:10

There may also be a misunderstanding in calculating years in the Jewish genealogy, as they used a different calendar, because archaeologists say they've discovered buildings dating back far longer than 2450 BC.

However, these older buildings may have been misdated, or they survived the transference from God's world in the flood into our world.

Can we use our common sense, constructive thinking, science, and the Bible to see if perhaps it is possible? Were these ancient buildings the construction of false gods or Cain's descendants performed on the destructed spiritual earth?

We saw our universe started somewhere else and was allowed to expand before our current physical realm or dimension existed.

It became a darkened sea, acting as God's junkyard, where the fallen angels, the fallen part of His earth, animals, and our corrupted spirit bodies eventually fell.

In other words, our universe was pre-made, perhaps for eons, in a different realm from a darkened and almost destroyed spiritual earth before it became our universe in our physical realm.

But do we have physical clues and evidence? Think about it. What do we do with items that are no longer useful, corrupted, or junk? Do we not throw them in the garbage and eventually to the dump, out of sight or away from our existence? Why do we recycle?

Don't we bury dead people in our earth, again, out of our sight and away from our existence?

We daily replicate many things on our earth that God already carried out, which is one way God proves His existence to us, through us. We do the same things He already accomplished.

Our Universe

Our universe was at one time a darkened sea, a dumping area for trillions of corrupted fallen beings, and a fallen earth. In many instances, the Bible equates stars with angels or the hosts of heaven.

Canst thou bind the sweet influences of Pleiades, or loose the bands of Orion?

Canst thou bring forth Mazzaroth in his season? or canst thou guide Arcturus with his sons?

Knowest thou the ordinances of heaven? canst thou set the dominion thereof in the earth?

–Job 38:31-33

And spiritual Lucifer, now Satan, is the ruler of our earth!

Does our universe appear as if it came from nothing, or instead, from substances from an enormous realm that flushed into the billions of bits and pieces we see as stars, planets, gases, etc.? If there was a big bang, it didn't blow up 'nothing'; it blew out the corrupted remnant spiritual earth as our universe.

But do our stars and planets look like they were once angels and spirit beings? To answer this, we only need to look at nature. Does an acorn look like it will become an oak tree?

Only after the acorn is buried in our earth does it become a new oak tree, and then it looks nothing like an acorn. This was a similar process for producing the hosts of our universe.

Would Noah have known the difference between a soon-to-be-destructed spiritual earth and our earth as he and his family and animals stepped off the ark? Probably not, other than there weren't the fallen gods in control again- yet.

Everything appears billions of years old to us from using physical laws looking backward instead of using spiritual laws looking forward from Genesis 1.

There is no longer darkness in the spirit realm, as it is all spiritual light. The remnant light left buried in the darkness is our physical light and is broken up into photons. Our universe is in a perpetual state of chaos, breaking down into deconstruction from the spirit realm.

Light is unbroken and instantaneous in God's world. It doesn't have to wobble or travel in waves on a darkened universal sea like it does in the physical realm.

In addition, all the spiritual world emits light, while nothing on our earth does, other than artificial light. Our bodies, animals, food, plants, or trees don't emit eternal light.

Scientists say they have discovered black holes in the center of galaxies. I don't think they realize yet how our entire universe is perhaps a black hole that started in the spiritual realm.

These black holes are supposedly swirling, sucking the galaxies into their darkened holes, sort of like enormous toilets. What if these trillions of black holes did the opposite (remember binary?) in centuries past and were fountains spewing the corrupted spiritual earth into our universe?

The stars and planets were already placed thousands of light years away from our earth in almost an instant when our universe began in our world. Most of their light was already stretched throughout the universe.

Thus shall ye say unto them, The gods that have not made the heavens and the earth, even they shall perish from the earth, and from under these heavens.

He hath made the earth by his power, he hath established the world by his wisdom, and hath stretched out the heavens by his discretion.

–Jeremiah 10:11-12

Part of the problem in interpreting the Genesis creation is we haven't allowed God to tell His story or for Him to be big enough.

The Lord's spiritual earth was spewed out from all the black holes forming the universe. When finished, the black holes reversed and will eventually flush our universe out of existence, leaving only the light of the spirit realm. Are these verses referring to this event?

But the day of the Lord will come as a thief in the night; in the which the heavens shall pass away with a great noise, and the elements shall melt with fervent heat, the earth also and the works that are therein shall be burned up.

Seeing then that all these things shall be dissolved, what manner of persons ought ye to be in all holy conversation and godliness,

Looking for and hasting unto the coming of the day of God, wherein the heavens being on fire shall be dissolved, and the elements shall melt with fervent heat?

Nevertheless we, according to his promise, look for new heavens and a new earth, wherein dwelleth righteousness.

–2 Peter 3:10–13

When the end comes, it will be sudden. Our physical universe will instantly disappear, and the spiritual realm will once again be our new home.

There won't be any warning of a rapture, antichrist, or seven-year tribulation. The end will come like a thief in the night. In the next instant, we could be standing in front of Jesus, and He either says:

"Welcome, my good and faithful servant." or

"Depart from me; I don't know you."

The last sentence holds the most frightening words in all of eternity. Seek and know the Lord while you still can!

Ask, and it shall be given you; seek, and ye shall find; knock, and it shall be opened unto you:

For every one that asketh receiveth; and he that seeketh findeth; and to him that knocketh it shall be opened.

–Matthew 7:7-8

Background Information To Aid Our Vision Impairment

When the inspired Jewish scribes wrote the scriptures, they wrote the words together, right to left, without vowels. There also wasn't a separation of verse and chapter. When they were done writing on their lengths of papyrus, the scroll was rolled up into a titled "Book".

Bible chapters and verses weren't separated, necessarily to break into a different thought, until between the 13th and 16th centuries AD.

Therefore, there seem to be a few subtle mistakes as to when a new chapter or verse should begin, possibly caused by certain translators lacking the Spirit of God.

If we read from the end of Genesis chapter 1—into chapter 2—it should become obvious, the Genesis 2:4 verse should have been the start of chapter 2. It closes Chapter 1 and introduces us to a different viewpoint, this time from the Lord God.

This would make the following verse:

And God blessed the seventh day, and sanctified it: because that in it he had rested from all his work which God created and made.

–Genesis 2:3

…the end of Chapter 1 created and made. Verse, 2:4, would become the first verse in chapter 2 with the Lord God and made…

These are the generations of the heavens and of the earth when they were created, in the day that the Lord God made the earth and the heavens...

Do we see the transition? It is again closing out the chapter 1 summary, restoration of God's world, into chapter 2—the Lord God making our earth and heavens. We have missed this transcendence from "God created and made" to "Lord God" simply "made".

In addition, if we refer to the Hebrew translation, please note the Bible sentences seem jumbled because they are structured as verb, noun, and object. For example, Genesis 1:1 translated from Hebrew and written as follows:

"In the beginning created God the heaven and the earth."

Created=verb, God=noun, heaven and earth=object.

By reading it this way, we might assume this thing called "In the beginning" created God, the heaven and the earth, instead of created as an action from God.

Newer Bibles didn't always follow what the inspired writers wrote. We already saw where the words vault and sky were erroneously used for firmament and heaven.

Some newer translators also translated the Genesis 2:4 word "generations" as "account". It is understood there is more than identifying the generations in Genesis, but account is not what was meant, and generations is the better translation in use for chapters 1-6. Otherwise, we might not see the regeneration or generations in the rest of the creation chapters.

These errors have caused us not to see the regeneration of God's kingdom in chapter 1 or the generational making of our earth and heavens in chapters 2–6, or how they reflect in Genesis 1.[6]

Let's take a closer look at this chapter 2:4 verse.

---

[6] If readers want to know more about why certain newer Bibles have purposely changed words, omitted words, or verses, please read the eBook: "7 Things to Know About the Bible. Why so many Bibles?"

"These are the generations of the heavens and of the earth when they were created, in the day that the Lord God made the earth and the heavens…"

What we need to look at is why the second part of the verse is stated somewhat in a mirrored fashion to the first part of the verse.

We've always been told, the first chapter of the Book of Genesis is the beginning of our earth, space, and time—all created in six days.

There isn't a doubt our physical realm was made in six days, our time, or perhaps eons in the spirit realm, because there is another reference to six days in the Bible (Exodus 20:11).

In chapter 7, the flood first mentions 7 days. Admittedly, it is still a struggle to determine if this is a reference to the seven days in Genesis 1. Or, is this the preparation ahead of making our universe, space, time, and physical earth, and flooding our universe and earth into a physical realm?

It seems, again, we have to look at the parallel created and made or restoration and making in the same instance, or "in the Day". What happens instantaneously in the spirit realm processes through time for us. However, it took over a year for everything to settle on our earth after the flood, transferring our universe into physical existence.

Genesis 2:4 is an interesting verse, reflecting what the Lord God did during or after God used the firmament to restore His kingdom. He is *making* what will become our physical realm from the aftermath of God's original *created* heaven and earth.

This 2:4 verse is like a demarcation point, where the responsibility ends on one side, God, and the other side, Lord God, takes over.

It is somewhat similar to a power company running electrical lines to our house, but an electrician takes over from the power pole or demarcation point the responsibility of installing the wiring throughout the house.

God's restored earth is let, made, and created as the Lord God made our earth and formed everything else.

There is a period, "in the day", within the created heavens and earth, and making the earth and heavens show us the events in the day as the spiritual realm.

Since there is not a strict reference to time because it is the spirit realm, this "day" could be eons in eternity—from the original creation of His kingdom to when it was almost destroyed in darkness and when the Lord God made our universe and earth. It only says "in the day", referencing the spirit realm.

The Jewish scribes used the word yom to describe the day in Genesis. Translators argue whether this is a twelve-hour or twenty-four-hour day. However, yom can be used for different meanings, including age.

As we saw in Genesis 1, the night is not in the spirit realm, as God defines a day as evening and morning, without night. Day is always in existence in God's kingdom. We should prefer God's translation, as He is dividing out the events of His restoration in His day in the spiritual realm.

Isaac Newton said, "For every action, there is an equal and opposite reaction." We, and our physical realm, currently exist as a reaction to the actions of God. Just as the timeless eternal realm will go on in timelessness, our physical realm, as a binary effect, will soon run out of time and dissolve into nothingness.

Something took a terrible turn in God's eternal kingdom. It is after this verse, 2:4, and the remaining formulating chapters and verses that we learn what happened.

Adam disobeyed God and brought the darkness of man's sin into existence in our spiritual lives.

Certain spiritual beings, sons of God, had already brought in their sin of rebellion and had intercourse with the spiritual women. (Genesis, chapter 6)

The Lord made our soul pure, but we corrupted it. It isn't our body that sins or rebels against God; it is our soul within our spirit.

This is what needs changing by repenting and cleansing through the shed blood of Jesus.

Once God has spiritually created something, it can never be completely destroyed. It can be modified, formed, or made; restored or recycled; dissolved into something else; but it is never altogether destroyed. Therefore, our spirit's conscious soul goes on forever in eternity, and our physical bodies dissolve back into dust.

If we can keep this understanding in the back of our minds, we will more easily grasp the creation story. We can't see how the creation story all happened in an instant because we are stuck in the movement of time. If we get back to heaven, we can see history all at once.

Thus, when Genesis 2:4 says, "These are the generations… in the Day" please understand that God creating His heaven and earth, Lucifer and His band of fellow rebellions bringing the earth to darkness waters, God restoring His world, and the Lord God forming our earth and universe, all happened "in the day" or at once in the spiritual realm.

Therefore, we can only experience it through God's words and Spirit, explaining the spiritual details, and we know the Lord God made our temporary physical realm and God restored His eternal earth for us. This is the alternate creation story in a nutshell.

God named a being in the spiritual realm Lucifer, which means 'light-bearer'. This might seem obvious, as all spiritual beings emit light, with God's light as the source, empowering other beings. According to the Orthodox Jewish Bible, he was called "Bright One of the Dawn, Day Star, Lucifer." (Isaiah 14:12, OJB)

He was apparently the most beautiful of all beings, and probably through jealousy, he thought he could establish his own light without God. By doing so through rebellion, he introduced darkness and deception to the other beings. He was cut off from God's source of light, along with every being who rebelled against God. We know if we turn off the light, there is darkness.

Lucifer was a beautiful cherub, but through his rebellion, he changed into a dragon-type serpent.

Thou hast been in Eden the garden of God; every precious stone was thy covering, the sardius, topaz, and the diamond, the beryl, the onyx, and the jasper, the sapphire, the emerald, and the carbuncle, and gold: the workmanship of thy tabrets and of thy pipes was prepared in thee in the day that thou wast created.

Thou art the anointed cherub that covereth; and I have set thee so: thou wast upon the holy mountain of God; thou hast walked up and down in the midst of the stones of fire.

Thou wast perfect in thy ways from the day that thou wast created, till iniquity was found in thee.

–Ezekiel 28:13-15

This light-bearer lost his light and became darkness, or the binary effect of God's light.

The theme from Job chapters 38–40 describes the making of our earth and life upon it by the Lord God. This is why Job should be read with Genesis, as it reveals more evidence about the creation story. It is apparent, Job was a descendant of Seth's line, dealing with false gods.

The spirit realm originally existed in perfect harmony with many diverse beings. After the rebellion of Lucifer, everything was changing into a binary effect. Good became evil, health brought sickness, faith into fear, life into death, etc. The binary effects of God passed into our universe and lives. But as we already know:

And He that sat upon the throne said, Behold I make all things new.

–Revelation 21:5

The Lord God Forms Man to Continue the Restoration

Where we are in the creation story, God has restored His earth and heaven. Now, He wants someone to continue the restoration. We saw the steps God would take to restore males and females—let, make, and create in His image and likeness.

The Lord God will start the process to form man from "dust" from the 'without form and void' earth. Since this is still the spiritual earth, it will be spiritual dust, called flesh.

In this portion of the Bible, flesh is a spiritual word; it is what a spirit body consists of, holding our soul. Flesh later changed into a physical skin to block Adam and Eve's sins from God's sight and presence. However, when we die, our spirit body will once again be flesh.

God's plan was to form a being who could receive His righteousness and holiness to continue what He had started. He would get Adam familiar with what he was supposed to do by starting out in a garden in God's kingdom.

Within the garden would be the Tree of Life for Adam to commune with and receive eternal life. We saw the garden was already in God's restored kingdom and will be used as a nursery to fill His earth.

It isn't clear whether Adam knew he was in God's kingdom, or at least an extension of it, but he was in close proximity to see everything. The Garden of Eden was a portal between God's kingdom, and the fallen earth.

However, this man would have to choose to do what God wanted in order to receive His eternal image and likeness.

Therefore, Adam received free will to do or not do God's will. He would have to give his complete allegiance to God and not to any other being.

The Lord God begins providing the restored earth with its needs, starting with man made from dust from the destructed earth. But first, Adam will have to be 'qualified'.

Let's continue the alternate creation story with the next verses, starting from Genesis 2:5, in our journey from the previous Genesis 2:4 verse:

And every plant of the field before it was in the earth, and every herb of the field before it grew: for the Lord God had not caused it to rain upon the earth, and there was not a man to till the ground.

–Genesis 2:5

Despite what we've been told from ancient teaching that Genesis, chapter 2, is a chronological continuation of the beginning story in chapter 1, we have seen this isn't the case.

What we are reading is there wasn't a plant or herb of the field in the earth, and no man yet. The creation story starts again, this time from the Lord's perspective!

We can perhaps see the field or ground was outside of Eden. In this argument, of course, there wasn't anything growing yet or man outside of God's kingdom—just the false or fallen gods.

There is a difference between the garden of Eden and the land outside of Eden. Adam, whom the Lord God is about to form, was to use these garden plants to begin the restoration after he ate from the

Tree of Life. This would have given Adam the image and likeness, or Spirit, of the Son or the Lord God-Jesus to exist for eternity with God.

God plans the best for us, but He also provides for us when we go against His will or make mistakes.

But there went up a mist from the earth, and watered the whole face of the ground.

And the Lord God formed man of the dust of the ground, and breathed into his nostrils the breath of life; and man became a living soul.

–Genesis 2: 6-7

The words "living soul" are two more words we've skimmed over. These words mean living within living, or a soul is combined with the breath of God.

It is the life difference between what animates animals and man. Animals have a breath of life, but it is different when God passes it into us. God did not breathe His type of spirit life into the nostrils of animals. We lost God's soul breath when we rebelled against Him.

For that which befalleth the sons of men befalleth beasts; even one thing befalleth them: as the one dieth, so dieth the other; yea, they have all one breath; so that a man hath no preeminence above a beast: for all is vanity.

All go unto one place; all are of the dust, and all turn to dust again.

Who knoweth the spirit of man that goeth upward, and the spirit of the beast that goeth downward to the earth?

–Ecclesiastes 3:19-21

We saw in Genesis 1, the spirits of animals are raised from the land. When we die, we go to God, but dead animals need to be raised from the land. What people have preconceived is God formed a physical man and animals. It doesn't say Adam is a physical or spiritual man with a physical or spiritual body, but a living soul with God's breath.

We understand, before anything else, we are all living souls, and this is what animates the spirit and physical body with life.

However, Adam is in spiritual flesh. For us, flesh forms temporary skin. He and Eve will be given skin later to cover their spiritual sins.

And the Lord God planted a garden eastward in Eden; and there he put the man whom he had formed.

And out of the ground made the Lord God to grow every tree that is pleasant to the sight, and good for food; the tree of life also in the midst of the garden, and the tree of knowledge of good and evil.

–Genesis 2:5-9

This is the same ground used to form Adam. Since God had to place Adam in the garden, it also implies He had to place the plants from outside of Eden into the garden. It is in this arena—where the challenge is made to Adam and Eve.

Before we go further, we should know Jesus, as the Lord God, made everything for us from our earth. Some readers might be disturbed by calling the Lord God, Jesus. However, when we read in John, chapter 1, and other verses, it shows He is.

In the beginning was the Word, and the Word was with God, and the Word was God.

The same was in the beginning with God.

All things were made by him; and without him was not any thing made that was made.

–John 1:1-3

Here again, we see how the Bible trips up false doctrines. This time, for those who state that Jesus is not God. The Word, Jesus, is the Lord God, who made everything.

The Word of God, the action from God, accomplished the making of all things as the Lord God.

It doesn't say He created anything, but we saw and now know He made everything out of already-created ingredients.

This garden is in a spiritual place called Eden. By observing the Tree of the Knowledge of Good and Evil and the Tree of Life, we could easily infer the other trees also had attributes.

The serpent appears to represent the good and evil knowledge tree, so the other trees perhaps were beings of righteousness or to draw Adam and Eve's attention toward the Tree of Life.

To appoint unto them that mourn in Zion, to give unto them beauty for ashes, the oil of joy for mourning, the garment of praise for the spirit of heaviness; that they might be called trees of righteousness, the planting of the Lord, that he might be glorified.

–Isaiah 61:3

It doesn't mention Adam or Eve communed with the other trees, or otherwise we might not be on our fallen earth today.

There is more to the story, which apparently most people haven't noticed or ignored, just as we didn't read or understand Genesis 1 accurately.

We see the Lord God made the earth and heavens, the plants and herbs, before they were in the earth. It is because it hadn't rained yet and there wasn't a man to till the ground.

If Adam had eaten or communed with the Tree of Life, he would have been the immediate first male-female restored in God's image and likeness to restore God's earth with these plants.

Later, we do discover he was the first male-female, after man called upon the Lord.

Without getting too literal, there is a difference between earth, ground, and dust.

Earth is the planet; ground is the destructed or ground-up part of the earth; and dust, without water, is a waste of ground. It is like coffee beans.

We don't drink the beans until they are shelled and the beans are dried and ground up into coffee grounds. We pour water onto the coffee grounds to enable us to drink coffee.

Earth is a planet of rocks. Once the rocks are dissolved, they become ground. Ground is ground because it is ground from our planet Earth. Dust results from dried, grounded earth, which is useless as waste without water, which is why there was mist outside of Eden.

What is shown here is the man was formed from the dust of the ground outside of Eden and blended with the mist. Apparently, if scientists think they can create life, they have to first get some dust and mist as spiritual flesh from the spirit realm. Then, figure out how to get God to breathe into the flesh to make a living soul.

Adam, at his formation, wasn't a physical body but had spiritual dust or flesh. This flesh can function in the spirit realm and originally emitted light. Whereas Lucifer and the fallen gods, no longer had light. This is one reason Lucifer, as the serpent, was jealous and wanted to remove Adam's light to rebel against God.

Adam's soul came to a spiritual life, which occurs at the end of the verse where the Lord God "breathed into his nostrils the breath of life; and man became a living soul."

Notice, it doesn't say he became a living physical body. This is what we are—living souls, not living bodies—but our soul gives us life and empowers our body.

Our living soul also gives us the ability to experience and know God. It is like an invisible, umbilical light tied from within us to God. We might call it consciousness.

However, the soul of Adam was alive in a vaporous, misty, or transparent spirit body. He needed to eat from the Tree of Life to obtain his spiritual completeness in the likeness and image of God and exist for eternity.

There is only one other time when the Lord God breathed into man, and it was at Pentecost when Jesus breathed His Spirit into his disciple's internal spirit bodies.

And when he had said this, he breathed on them, and saith unto them, Receive ye the Holy Ghost:

–John 20:22

This, in effect, rekindled the disciple's internal spirit body, where they and we became born again, just as the Lord God here is kindling Adam to become a born spiritual soul, to function with God.

Thus, Adam started out as a living soul, within a spirit body covering a type of framed physical body. His spirit body emitted a divine spiritual light from his soul, which the Jews called Shikinah Glory.

God formed Adam and Eve to continue the restoration of His kingdom. When God breathes or immerses His Spirit of Fire into us to become born again, we will join all the others in white-robed spirit bodies and resume restoring His kingdom.

After this I beheld, and, lo, a great multitude, which no man could number, of all nations, and kindreds, and people, and tongues, stood before the throne, and before the Lamb, clothed with white robes, and palms in their hands;

–Revelation 7:9

White robes mean our souls are purified again. The palms might mean, symbolically, the harvest is over on our earth, or we are ready to go to work in God's kingdom.

Originally, we were never meant to be on our physical earth but were to remain in God's kingdom, eventually moving into His restored kingdom out of the garden after eating from the Tree of Life. Eating from the Tree of Life is symbolic of God's eternal plan of salvation through Jesus.

For my flesh is meat indeed, and my blood is drink indeed.

He that eateth my flesh, and drinketh my blood, dwelleth in me, and I in him.

–John 6:56-57

We know this is spiritually speaking and we don't literally eat His spiritual flesh and drink His physical blood, but do so symbolically in communion with Him. We become intertwined with Jesus and we receive His spirit. This is when we are made in the image and likeness of God.

It is the spirit that quickeneth; the flesh profiteth nothing: the words that I speak unto you, they are spirit, and they are life.

–John 6:63

The spirit realm with God comes alive when we view verses from God's wisdom and images, and not from our preconceived ideas of understanding.

The Garden

After Adam receives His living soul, the next verse has three important terms: Garden, Eastward, and Eden, where we need to see the deeper translations.

And the LORD God planted a garden eastward in Eden; and there he put the man whom he had formed.

–Genesis 2:8

And the Lord God took the man, and put him into the garden of Eden to dress it and to keep it.

–Genesis 2:15

We skipped the rivers and land verses for now to continue the garden story.

Why does it specifically state the garden was planted eastward? Why does it say the Lord God put the man in the garden?

The first thing to note is the word eastward. Man has always looked at the east as where their gods are, or at least where the spirit realm abides. It is where the sun first appears, and some religions still worship the sunrise as a spiritual event.

We know the word 'eastward' means toward the east, and it does. But why would God specify He planted a garden eastward in Eden? Why was it important? If we dig a little deeper, eastward, in this Hebrew context is qedem, which means aforetime or time past, or 'before our time'.

This would help us verify these events are not happening on our current earth but in eternity before the existence of physical time.

There is no physical time yet in God's world, and therefore, all the activities are happening 'eastward' or before our time. We did read there is a type of spiritual time, such as days and years. It is different because physical time ticks out our sentence for rebelling against God. It began when Adam and Eve were banished from the garden. But in God's kingdom, days and years show how much of God's kingdom is restored.

This is perhaps difficult for our finite minds because we have to acknowledge there is a spiritual realm where there are additional things to learn.[7]

The garden translates as an enclosed garden. Walls are usually built to keep something out or in, for privacy, or to divide territory. It was God's garden, a place to grow perpetual herbs, plants, and trees to fill His restored kingdom. The wall kept others out, such as the false gods, and the garden was kept pure for His kingdom.

God put the man in the garden in Eden as an apprentice. The Lord formed man outside of Eden from the dust of the destroyed spiritual earth, and Adam could not get to the garden on his own because it was part of the restored kingdom of God. The Garden of Eden was not accessible by anyone outside of God's kingdom without God allowing it. It is why God had to put Adam in the garden.

It is the setting for a trial or challenge in an enclosed area to see how Adam and later Eve would function as potential God-man in His kingdom. The trial was between God and man, and the fallen gods could not interfere or see what was happening.

After all, God had never made a God-man and given him a living soul with a free will to receive God's eternal Spirit. This challenge could then be held to see if Adam and Eve and their descendants

---

[7] To know that we know what we know, and to know that we do not know what we do not know, that is true knowledge. - Nicolaus Copernicus

would restore God's earth, starting with a garden, without repeating or rebelling against God as the fallen angels had done.

We know Adam and Eve failed their trial, and when they lost the spirit breath of life, it meant they would eventually die, lose their light, or not be with God and would receive the same judgment as Lucifer and the fallen angels.

It appears God planned on their failure, which is why He made a temporary physical frame within their spirit body to function later in the physical realm if needed.

Time started measuring out our sentence after our soul disobeyed God, like a judge passes judgment on criminals for breaking laws, and the lawbreaker serves time in prison.

We are still passing through the judgment handed out to Adam, Eve, Cain, and his descendants today and are quarantined or imprisoned on our earth.

Therefore, no matter how great we think we are, we are all convicts until we are pardoned, saved, and restored by our Savior.

Can we see the spiritual image of why we have prisons?

Breaking Another Deception

When we read the Bible, our mind wants to place what we read in chronological order, and often this isn't the case. It is clear, starting in chapter 2:4, when we see the Lord God make the earth and the heavens, it is starting over with the creation story. [8]

When we left off, the Lord God had formed man, but interrupted His story to tell us about some rivers and land outside of Eden.

A river flowed out of the garden and divided into four major rivers, which provided the source of existence for the fallen beings outside of Eden. The rivers kept Cain and his descendants alive and would eventually provide the mineral resources after the flood, which are now found in the depths of our current earth.

Despite the fallen gods and man rebelling against God, He still provided for them—just as we provide for prisoners on death row until the end.

And a river went out of Eden to water the garden; and from thence it was parted, and became into four heads.

The name of the first is Pison: that is it which compasseth the whole land of Havilah, where there is gold;

---

[8] There is a chronological order of the OT in the Appendix at the back of this book.

the gold of that land is good: there is bdellium and the onyx stone.

And the name of the second river is Gihon: the same is it that compasseth the whole land of Ethiopia.

And the name of the third river is Hiddekel: that is it which goeth toward the east of Assyria. And the fourth river is Euphrates.

–Genesis 2:10-14

Some people claim they know where these rivers and lands are on our planet. But, as we've seen, they weren't here. Through bamboozling man in our history, the false gods deceived us into calling certain areas of our land and rivers the same names as areas where they ruled the spirit earth.

However, after the flood and centuries of planet upheavals and earthquakes, none of these original places or rivers could have survived.

God mentioned these rivers and places to show us there was an existence outside of the Garden and Eden, governed by fallen angels as false gods. A fallen man would also need to exist on the fallen earth.

The rivers would be necessary after God banned Cain from Eden to follow and continue their lives until death. The fallen gods, and our fallen spirits, would follow these rivers to the four ends of the fallen earth. Rivers and lands provide the ability to build cities and nations ruled by false gods.

Even though our nature is evil, God has still shown mercy to us through His stunning images of heaven as nature on our earth.

Therefore, God provides us with a blue atmosphere during the day—temporarily shielding us from the eternal darkness, showing there is light in the absence of darkness.

And the Lord God took the man, and put him into the garden of Eden to dress it and to keep it.

And the Lord God commanded the man, saying, Of every tree of the garden thou mayest freely eat:

But of the tree of the knowledge of good and evil, thou shalt not eat of it: for in the day that thou eatest thereof thou shalt surely die.

And the Lord God said, It is not good that the man should be alone; I will make him an help meet for him.

And out of the ground the Lord God formed every beast of the field, and every fowl of the air; and brought them unto Adam to see what he would call them: and whatsoever Adam called every living creature, that was the name thereof.

And Adam gave names to all cattle, and to the fowl of the air, and to every beast of the field; but for Adam there was not found a help meet for him.

And the Lord God caused a deep sleep to fall upon Adam, and he slept: and he took one of his ribs, and closed up the flesh instead thereof;

And the rib, which the Lord God had taken from man, made he a woman, and brought her unto the man.

–Genesis 2:15-22

It is clear, God put Adam in charge of the garden and of the animals within. It seems the smaller animals were brought into the garden, and the larger beasts were left in the field. Adam is beginning his apprenticeship into the dominion of the new heaven and earth.

It was already explained that God 'let' the animals out of the land in Chapter 1. This ties in with the Lord God formed the animals from the ground, the land or field outside of Eden, to be restored in God's kingdom. However, there weren't the thousands of different animal species we have today.

There were probably what we now call dinosaurs, or previous dragons, along with the other primary beasts such as leviathans, mammoths, saber-toothed tigers, wolves, primates, and so forth. They were called beasts. No puppies or kittens yet.

All the 'lower' species of animals mutated or decreated from these greater beasts on our earth.

The garden was initially to feed the animals and man, who would later distribute the plants, herbs, and trees throughout the kingdom. The animals would help in the distribution.

The garden was the training ground for man to go into the rest of the restored earth to care for the plants and animals, if he wouldn't rebel against God as other beings did.

Despite some people thinking all they need are pets as companions, it seems to prove here that we need the opposite gender person to interact with.

The verses say the Lord took a rib out of Adam to form Eve. We know the ribs are the center portion, the life-supporting section of a body, between the head and the legs.

The rib is spiritually symbolic, as He took the center portion of man, or the womb, out of Adam, along with the female hormones, in order to form Eve. Therefore, the female are called womb-man or women because the female and feminine attributes were removed from man.

And Adam said, This is now bone of my bones, and flesh of my flesh: she shall be called Woman, because she was taken out of Man.

Therefore shall a man leave his father and his mother, and shall cleave unto his wife: and they shall be one flesh.

And they were both naked, the man and his wife, and were not ashamed.

–Genesis 2:23-25

Now, we know the word flesh here refers to the spirit body, and we can see the spiritual meaning that the Lord used part of Adam's physical frame to form Eve.

This verse confirms the inner physical womb of Adam was taken out of his spirit body, or "bone of my bones, and flesh of my flesh," and the woman was given a spirit body.

When a man and woman marry, they do not literally become one physical person. They do become one spirit of flesh, at least in the eyes of God. It is what is meant by male-female restoration. Therefore, divorce is frowned upon by God, as it breaks the planned spiritual union of the male-female.

Part of Adam's framing, innards, with spirit flesh covering, formed Eve. It doesn't say the Lord breathed life into her or that she also became a living soul. This means the soul in a newborn comes through the man.

Since they had not sinned yet or rebelled against God, they were still emanating their light, or Shekinah Glory, and didn't know or see the shame of sin as nakedness before each other or God.

The Devil Made Me Do It

Now the serpent was more subtil than any beast of the field which the Lord God had made. And he said unto the woman, Yea, hath God said, Ye shall not eat of every tree of the garden?

And the woman said unto the serpent, We may eat of the fruit of the trees of the garden:

But of the fruit of the tree which is in the midst of the garden, God hath said, Ye shall not eat of it, neither shall ye touch it, lest ye die.

And the serpent said unto the woman, Ye shall not surely die:

For God doth know that in the day ye eat thereof, then your eyes shall be opened, and ye shall be as gods, knowing good and evil.

–Genesis 3:1-5

The serpent was probably a dragon, or Lucifer changed into a seraph from a cherub after he rebelled, which looked like a dragon and not a snake.

This passage shows, the serpent possessed a higher level of subtlety or craftiness. It means, as Lucifer, he determined how to trick Eve, Adam, and later Cain, stealing away their allegiance toward God.

From the old school creation teaching, Bible teachers taught us the serpent was a talking snake. This makes little sense, as we will soon see.

It was seemingly a dragon-type serpent from Job 41, in which the Bible would later describe Satan as having the nature of a dragon.

The other thing to note that nobody seemed to consider is Eve wasn't afraid of the dragon or shocked because the serpent could speak! It is apparent all animals, including dragons, were at least friendly and could talk in the garden and in God's kingdom. It is also obvious; the Lord allowed the dragon into the garden.

The next strange thing is, Eve tells the serpent, "God hath said, Ye shall not eat of it neither shall ye touch it, lest ye die."

Our Bible doesn't say they couldn't touch it, but that Adam couldn't eat from the tree. It could be when Adam showed Eve around the garden and they came upon this tree; Adam said God explained to him not to eat from it. Thus, maybe Adam told Eve, "So don't go near it or even touch it," displaying a bit of the authority given to him in the garden.

The serpent gives her his deception, a morsel of truth, but does not imply the destruction involved. This is how deception works: tell somebody enough truth so they believe you, and you can tack on the destruction or achieve your way with the deception. It is how leaders in our world work.

The bit of truth from the serpent was, she wouldn't die by touching the fruit. She might not even die from eating the fruit, since God only told Adam not to eat. She and Adam might have been able to feel the fruit and juggle it to their hearts' content without a judgment from God.

The serpent tells her they will be like gods, knowing both good and evil, as if this were a good thing, as the fallen gods knew both good and evil, to their destruction.

And when the woman saw that the tree was good for food, and that it was pleasant to the eyes, and a tree to be desired to

make one wise, she took of the fruit thereof, and did eat, and gave also unto her husband with her; and he did eat.

And the eyes of them both were opened, and they knew that they were naked; and they sewed fig leaves together, and made themselves aprons.

–Genesis 3:6-7

Some religions teach the fruit was toxic and that it affected our genes, so we die. There was probably nothing wrong with the tree or the fruit itself, as it provided shelter for the animals.

It was the shifting of allegiance from God to the devil that caused their spiritual deaths.

The following verses may describe Lucifer as the symbolic tree before his fall.

All the fowls of heaven made their nests in his boughs, and under his branches did all the beasts of the field bring forth their young, and under his shadow dwelt all great nations.

Thus was he fair in his greatness, in the length of his branches: for his root was by great waters.

The cedars in the garden of God could not hide him: the fir trees were not like his boughs, and the chestnut trees were not like his branches; nor any tree in the garden of God was like unto him in his beauty.

I have made him fair by the multitude of his branches: so that all the trees of Eden, that were in the garden of God, envied him.

–Ezekiel 31:6-9

Eve perhaps saw animals eat from the tree and was taken in by its beauty. She hadn't sinned yet, and touching or eating the fruit probably wasn't her transgression. It was the rebellion of Adam toward God that brought about their eternal demise.

Only after Adam ate from the tree did they know the nakedness of their sin toward each other. They no longer emitted their spiritual glory and tried to hide their exposed sin from God with fig leaves.

It wasn't the fruit that caused their and our destruction. It was purposely rebelling against God.

The point was, would man obey the Lord God in the garden and not commit sin or rebel?

Every time we sin, it is our inner spirit or soul rebelling against God. We've become like Satan's fallen gods.

Our conscious soul pings us each time we steal a cookie from the cookie jar. We stand naked before God in our shame as we try to bury the knowledge of our wrongdoing in self-righteousness while we suffer the consequences.

We turn away from God, hiding our sin from Him, just as Adam and Eve did. We don't want it exposed to others, and we put on our robes of self-righteousness to guard it from others finding us out.

Disobeying God steeps us in shame and guilt, and we don't want to be held personally accountable for our actions.

The Denial and Judgment

As we read the following scriptures, we see Adam and Eve refused to be held accountable for their actions. Instead, they played a blame game on God, each other, and the serpent. There is one word or action missing from Adam and Eve toward God—repentance.

And they heard the voice of the Lord God walking in the garden in the cool of the day: and Adam and his wife hid themselves from the presence of the Lord God amongst the trees of the garden.

And the Lord God called unto Adam, and said unto him, Where art thou?

And he said, I heard thy voice in the garden, and I was afraid, because I was naked; and I hid myself.

And he said, Who told thee that thou wast naked? Hast thou eaten of the tree, whereof I commanded thee that thou shouldest not eat?

And the man said, The woman whom thou gavest to be with me, she gave me of the tree, and I did eat.

And the Lord God said unto the woman, What is this that thou hast done? And the woman said, The serpent beguiled me, and I did eat.

–Genesis 3:9-13

We saw in the previous chapter how they made fig leaves to cover themselves. This might be comical if it wasn't so tragic.

Here, they hid themselves within the trees, obviously fig trees, hoping they would blend in and God wouldn't see their shame and guilt with their covering camouflage.

After they disobeyed God, they became self-conscious with shame instead of God-conscious. They became self-righteous, wanting God to look past their guilt in what they did, as if it wasn't their fault.

First, Adam blames God for giving him the woman. The woman then blames the serpent. Neither one admitted their fault for disobeying God. They attempted to hide their exposed guilt and shame with fig leaves and blend in with the trees of righteousness.

And the Lord God said unto the serpent, Because thou hast done this, thou art cursed above all cattle, and above every beast of the field; upon thy belly shalt thou go, and dust shalt thou eat all the days of thy life:

And I will put enmity between thee and the woman, and between thy seed and her seed; it shall bruise thy head, and thou shalt bruise his heel.

–Genesis 3:14-15

According to these verses, the serpent was larger or smarter than the cattle or beasts, and therefore, the curse is above cattle and beasts. Bible readers have thought the serpent was a snake, but we see the curse is for it to be on its belly and to eat dust.

If it was a snake, then this wasn't much of a curse, as a snake did this already, unless it wasn't a snake to begin with. The evidence shows the serpent was a dragon, or Leviathan.

However, what crawls on its belly and constantly eats dust? A worm.

(Worm excerpt definition from the Merriam-Webster dictionary: "... being who is an object of contempt, loathing, or pity: something that torments or devours from within: to proceed or make (one's way) insidiously or deviously.)"

Doesn't this definition describe Satan?

Did the Lord God mutate a dragon into a worm, and is the devil now a worm? Isn't this his description from hell?

Where their worm dieth not, and the fire is not quenched.

–Mark 9:46

It makes more sense to think of Lucifer-Satan, the devil, as a worm.

The Lord God said he would put enmity, or hatred, between the serpent's seed and the woman's. It is through faith and righteousness toward God that she will continue to bruise the worm's head.

Unto the woman he said, I will greatly multiply thy sorrow and thy conception; in sorrow thou shalt bring forth children; and thy desire shall be to thy husband, and he shall rule over thee.

–Genesis 3:16

Eve's judgment is sorrowful, perhaps, for disobeying Adam, who apparently told her not to touch the tree, but also because she will have to look toward Adam for his seed of a living soul. Thus, if a woman wants a child, she will always have to desire a man to give her one.

This may not have been the case if they had not sinned. God would have directly made us in His image and likeness through His Spirit. Jesus is the image and likeness of God, and now He can restore us as such.

And unto Adam he said, Because thou hast hearkened unto the voice of thy wife, and hast eaten of the tree, of which I commanded thee, saying, Thou shalt not eat of it: cursed is the ground for thy sake; in sorrow shalt thou eat of it all the days of thy life;

Thorns also and thistles shall it bring forth to thee; and thou shalt eat the herb of the field;

In the sweat of thy face shalt thou eat bread, till thou return unto the ground; for out of it wast thou taken: for dust thou art, and unto dust shalt thou return.

And Adam called his wife's name Eve; because she was the mother of all living.

–Genesis 3:14-20

Adam and Eve most likely never had to work for their food in the garden. It constantly regenerated the fruits and vegetables, or whatever they desired to consume.

Now, they are stuck eating bread made from thorns, thistles, and herbs and have to go outside of Eden to the field to get it from the ground.

Adam-Man constantly has to work to support himself and his family. It will be a continual source of frustration, thorns, and thistles as our soul reminds us of our failure in the garden. We still eat bread until we die.

Unto Adam also and to his wife did the Lord God make coats of skins, and clothed them.

–Genesis 3:21

Although the Bible does not mention it, people often assume God sacrificed animals to create clothing for Adam and Eve. Instead, it seems more likely; it was the first time we had coats of physical skin. Admittedly, it is difficult to explain the mode of action here.

As mentioned before, Adam and Eve first had a divine covering called flesh. After they sinned, this covering disappeared, and their spirit bodies exposed their fallen spiritual attributes.

God brought physical skin to life over their spirit bodies to hide their sins; otherwise, the righteousness of God would have vaporized them away from God. So far, the Lord God has made all things from the dust of the earth, and therefore, it doesn't seem difficult to believe He made skin the same way.

We don't sin physically; we sin spiritually. Yes, we can be thieves, and the action is performed physically, but our body doesn't care or know what it is doing. However, it is exposing the sin nature in our spirit.

We still have skin covering our body. We cannot see guilt, shame, fear, and other fallen spiritual characteristics in ours or others' bodies.

Everyone has a consciousness of God and of doing His will or evil in their soul, whether or not they will admit it. If not, we would never know when we rebel against God.

And the Lord God said, Behold, the man is become as one of us, to know good and evil: and now, lest he put forth his hand, and take also of the tree of life, and eat, and live for ever:

Therefore the Lord God sent him forth from the garden of Eden, to till the ground from whence he was taken.

So he drove out the man; and he placed at the east of the garden of Eden Cherubim, and a flaming sword which turned every way, to keep the way of the tree of life.

–Genesis 3:22-24

The verse means, if they had gone to the Tree of Life now in their fallen state or without repentance, they would have lived in darkness, knowing good and evil for eternity as fallen gods—no pathway for restoration thereafter.

The implication was that they were to do this first, to be with God forever on His restored earth. To whom would they show their allegiance—God or someone else? They chose Lucifer, the fallen worm.

The Lord casts them out of the garden, but not Eden, and physical time begins because they are no longer in the kingdom of God. It seems they could still live in Eden but have to go outside into the realm of the false gods to till the ground for food.

Regardless, eternity with God is behind them, and no one can get to the Tree of Life or become restored male-female, as in Genesis 1, until man calls upon the name of the Lord. Their lives will continue in Eden or outside on the dust of the ground until they die.

East of Eden

Unfortunately, we probably don't realize it yet, but most of us are still, symbolically, living east of Eden. It is where Lucifer, functioning as a worm and deceiving the nations, has jurisdiction over the earth, along with all the fallen angels, with the chaos and destruction they are bringing upon the Lord God's spiritual earth.

This was life on our soon-to-be earth, where our souls would be born as Cain's descendants, under the deception of Lucifer and the rule of the false gods. It is difficult to understand the love God still had for us, and even after we still turn away from Him.

According as he hath chosen us in him before the foundation of the world, that we should be holy and without blame before him in love:

Having predestinated us unto the adoption of children by Jesus Christ to himself, according to the good pleasure of his will,

–Ephesians 1:4-5

Despite His ability to leave us in eternal darkness, Jesus adopts us back into His kingdom.

Until then, this is who governed our spiritual lives.

Thy pomp is brought down to the grave, and the noise of thy viols: the worm is spread under thee, and the worms cover thee.

How art thou fallen from heaven, O Lucifer, son of the morning! how art thou cut down to the ground, which didst weaken the nations!

... Yet thou shalt be brought down to hell, to the sides of the pit.

They that see thee shall narrowly look upon thee, and consider thee, saying, Is this the man that made the earth to tremble, that did shake kingdoms;

That made the world as a wilderness, and destroyed the cities thereof; that opened not the house of his prisoners?

–Isaiah 14:11-12, 15-17

This is a deeper look into Genesis 1:2, east of Eden. In these verses, the worm, shown as Lucifer, includes the fallen angels, also described as worms because they are from his 'seed' of evil. The second verse says he fell from heaven and was cut down to the ground, verifying he was the worm east of Eden.

Last, the verses infer he was leading the rebellion, holding everyone under his spell. We spent ages in the spirit realm destroying the earth, just as we have done for ages now on our earth. What other witness do we need?

We are causing animals to go extinct, poisoning our and their food with toxic chemicals, creating new viruses, polluting our rivers and oceans, killing off sea creatures, indirectly funding demonic-controlled terrorists as false gods so they can kill off millions of people, and so on and so on. Is it truly too difficult to see we are repeating what we did in a past life?

However, after reading these last Bible verses, they show the spiritual events that brought us to our world. We didn't have a talking serpent turn into a worm, cherubs, a flaming sword, or a garden of Eden with a tree of good and evil or a tree of life on our current earth. These were all spiritual events happening in a different world.

No one has caused our world to become a wilderness yet, but it will happen.

Here is how God's earth looked after the destruction from the fallen gods when God gave the prophet Jeremiah a glimpse, expanding Genesis 1:2 again.

I beheld the earth, and, lo, it was without form, and void; and the heavens, and they had no light.

I beheld the mountains, and, lo, they trembled, and all the hills moved lightly.

I beheld, and, lo, there was no man, and all the birds of the heavens were fled.

I beheld, and, lo, the fruitful place was a wilderness, and all the cities thereof were broken down at the presence of the Lord, and by his fierce anger.

For thus hath the Lord said, The whole land shall be desolate; yet will I not make a full end.

For this shall the earth mourn, and the heavens above be black; because I have spoken it, I have purposed it, and will not repent, neither will I turn back from it.

–Jeremiah 4:23-28

Our heavens are black because they are the destructed spiritual earth-darkened waters. He is not yet ending everything because of evil. God has restored His new heaven and earth and flushed away all the destruction described in these verses, making our physical realm and mourning earth.

In the disciple's prayer (it isn't the Lord's prayer), it is stated,

"Thy kingdom come, thy will be done, in earth as it is in heaven."

–Matthew 6:10

The prayer promoted His resurrection and sent His Holy Spirit to exist within our spirit. His kingdom is here and now in fire-baptized disciples of Jesus, calling the world to repent into restoration with God.

Neither shall they say, Lo here! or, lo there! for, behold, the kingdom of God is within you.

–Luke 17:21

Some of us currently rule with the Spirit of God over the darkness on this earth.

And hath made us kings and priests unto God and his Father; to him be glory and dominion for ever and ever. Amen.

–Revelation 1: 6

Blessed and holy is he that hath part in the first resurrection: on such the second death hath no power, but they shall be priests of God and of Christ, and shall reign with him a thousand years.

–Revelation 20:6

When we are born again, we are in the first resurrection. We are in His "thousand-year" reign. This isn't a literal thousand years, as a thousand means infinite or without an exact number in the OT. So far, it's been going on for approximately 2000 years with His true church reigning on our earth as in heaven, through spirit-baptized Christians.

Jesus also said He was leaving to prepare a mansion for us (John 14:2–3). Why would He do this if He is to rule on our earth from a supposed rebuilt temple?

This is another deception handed down through the centuries. We will exist in His kingdom in the eternal realm when our physical bodies or realm dissolve. He will rule in His temple in heaven or on Mt. Zion, in the new Jerusalem, and we will rule on His earth.

Our existence on earth could end at any moment, "like a thief in the night." God will transcend some of us into His light of Day and the rest into darkness. Choose the light while we still can!

To Knew, The Birthing of a Soul

The creation story continues and exposes what happened in Eden after Adam rebelled against the Lord, eventually banishing them from the garden in God's kingdom.

Admittedly, we still need help from God's Spirit to determine what happened concerning relations in the spirit realm.

We discover how Eve had two sons, why Cain killed Abel, and there is a place called Nod outside of Eden. Cain gets kicked out of Eden for killing his brother and goes to Nod, east of Eden. There, he starts the Cain lineage, as opposed to the coming descendants from the Seth line in Eden.

Nod is further evidence showing us other beings, fallen angels, cities, and nations rebelled against God are outside of Eden.

Thus, to envision the images in the bigger picture:

There is the garden in the kingdom of God, which is no longer accessible until God restores man.

Eden is where the Lord rules, and Adam and Eve probably still live there. But Adam has to go to work outside of Eden to till the ground.

The rest of the world outside of Eden is where the fallen angels exist and rule on the ground with Lucifer, the worm. Next, the scene shifts back to Eden.

And Adam knew Eve his wife; and she conceived, and bare Cain, and said, I have gotten a man from the Lord.

And she again bare his brother Abel. And Abel was a keeper of sheep, but Cain was a tiller of the ground.

–Genesis 4:1-2

The word "knew" is used to produce Cain and Abel. Knew means what we think it does: having known someone or something. It is also a spiritual word, at least how God uses it in this context.

We can speculate about what happened by following the Lord's words in a previous chapter:

He made Adam a living soul. He has first made us a living soul. This is what the implied spiritual term "knew" means, because Eve said, "I have gotten, or acquired, a man from the Lord." It is apparent, she didn't have sex with the Lord but understood the spiritual process of making a soul. Therefore, living souls passed from the Lord through Adam into Eve and into Cain and Abel.

Before I formed thee in the belly I knew thee; and before thou camest forth out of the womb I sanctified thee, and I ordained thee a prophet unto the nations.

–Jeremiah 1:5

Some of the newer Bibles say Adam and Eve had sex. This is perhaps true, but they missed the point. In Jeremiah's verse, it says He knew us before we were born and formed us in a womb. This has to mean He knew us into a living soul as a spirit being before we became a physical being.

It is obvious He first made or "knew" us as a process into becoming eternal souls in a spirit body, currently within a physical body.

God places a name on our soul. It is our unique identification. Our parents make up a name for us, but when we return to the spirit realm, our soul name will become the one God gave us.

As evidence, God changed names in the OT, such as Abram to Abraham and Jacob to Israel, and in the NT, Jesus changed Simon's name to Peter, and Saul, the persecutor of the disciples, became Paul, the leader of the Gentile disciples. The name change includes all who receive and listen to the Spirit of God.

He that hath an ear, let him hear what the Spirit saith unto the churches; To him that overcometh will I give to eat of the hidden manna, and will give him a white stone, and in the stone a new name written, which no man knoweth saving he that receiveth it.

–Revelation 2:17

The spiritual learning presented in this book is perhaps the first time Bible readers have seen the hidden manna in His Word. When we hear what the Spirit is saying to us in His translation, the hidden manna will jump out of the verses into our hearts and minds with God's more profound spiritual wisdom.

The living soul would come from the seed of Adam, provided by the Lord, as it still does today. Perhaps Cain would have been the serpent-head-bruiser if he had not opposed God.

Lucifer had first deceived Adam and Eve and, likely, also Cain into disobedience. Cain tilled the land outside of Eden, and his brother raised animals in Eden.

And in process of time it came to pass, that Cain brought of the fruit of the ground an offering unto the Lord.

–Genesis 4:3

The first thing to note is this is the first mention of time or the process of time. It started when Adam and Eve got kicked out of the garden as unrepentant beings. They began their sentence of punishment outside the garden in Eden.

The Bible doesn't say why Cain first brought an offering to the Lord. We can infer from further scripture that it was to manipulate God in order to claim his first-born rights.

And Abel, he also brought of the firstlings of his flock and of the fat thereof.

–Genesis 4:4

It implies since Abel brought the firstlings, Cain, and Abel understood the first-born importance. Cain was the firstborn and would, therefore, have firstborn rights and perhaps get to rule Eden after Adam.

We get this from God later stating Cain would rule over Abel. Thus, Cain brought the offering, perhaps to urge God to give him his rights or to rule in Eden.

Abel followed his big brother's act, bringing his offering of animals from Eden and what they produced.

And the Lord had respect unto Abel and to his offering:

But unto Cain and to his offering he had not respect. And Cain was very wroth, and his countenance fell.

And the Lord said unto Cain, Why art thou wroth? and why is thy countenance fallen?

If thou doest well, shalt thou not be accepted? and if thou doest not well, sin lieth at the door. And unto thee shall be his desire, and thou shalt rule over him.

–Genesis 4:4-7

It appears the Lord didn't have a problem with Cain ruling over Abel. The thing to note is the Lord was still somewhere available to Cain and Abel, as they both brought Him an offering. This means they were still in or around Eden, where the Lord governed the land, probably with Adam and Eve. Therefore, it is clear the Lord was still talking with Adam and his family.

We see this in our world, too, as God's land is Israel, with the Jews at times ruling with God while surrounded by nations ruled by false gods—the same as we are now reading about the fallen spiritual world.

Cain first brought an offering from the cursed ground to the Lord. Since Adam caused the cursed ground, perhaps Cain thought the Lord would desire the first fruit of the ground. It may be Abel was closer to or interacted with the Lord and, therefore, understood the Lord better than Cain.

Abel also brings an offering to the Lord: the firstborn and fat from his animals, most likely the milk-fat from them.

Abel brings life before the Lord. Cain brings a curse to the Lord, a bucket full of dead weeds. Abel brought faith, and Cain brought an agenda.

By faith, Abel offered unto God a more excellent sacrifice than Cain, by which he obtained witness that he was righteous, God testifying of his gifts: and by it he being dead yet speaketh.

–Hebrews 11:4

This ticked Cain off; perhaps he expected the Lord would have respected him for simply being the firstborn. Abel wasn't the firstborn, but he brought the life of the firstborn of his animals.

Despite it all, the Lord told Cain that he was still in good standing as long as he does what is right—Abel will yet look up to him as his big brother, and Cain will lose nothing. He would still eventually rule with God in Eden and the descendants in Eden when Adam could no longer be with the Lord.

And Cain talked with Abel his brother: and it came to pass, when they were in the field, that Cain rose up against Abel his brother, and slew him.

–Genesis 4:8

We can imply that Cain led Abel out of Eden, away from the Lord, to the ground or field of the earth. It seems Cain listened to Lucifer or his false gods, and he killed off Abel.

Not as Cain, who was of that wicked one, and slew his brother. And wherefore slew he him? Because his own works were evil, and his brother's righteous.

–1 John 3:12

Perhaps Lucifer thought God chose Abel to be the serpent-head-bruising Lord, or at least the start of the seed lineage. With Abel gone, Cain believed God would have no choice but to acknowledge him as the ruler after Adam, and Lucifer could control him.

And the Lord said unto Cain, Where is Abel thy brother? And he said, I know not: Am I my brother's keeper?

And he said, What hast thou done? The voice of thy brother's blood crieth unto me from the ground.

–Genesis 4:9-10

God hears Abel's voice from the ground, another spiritual ability. Again, our body will die, but our soul never dies.

And now art thou cursed from the earth, which hath opened her mouth to receive thy brother's blood from thy hand;

When thou tillest the ground, it shall not henceforth yield unto thee her strength; a fugitive and a vagabond shalt thou be in the earth.

And Cain said unto the Lord, My punishment is greater than I can bear.

Behold, thou hast driven me out this day from the face of the earth; and from thy face shall I be hid; and I shall be a fugitive and a vagabond in the earth; and it shall come to pass, that every one that findeth me shall slay me.

–Genesis 4:11-14

We see the foundation building for the destruction of the spiritual earth. It wasn't just because the rebellious false gods were ruling; Adam fell under their spell, and now Cain. It gets worse.

If there wasn't existence outside of Eden, how could anyone in the earth slay Cain, or why was he afraid? Cain will lose protection from the Lord, so now he is afraid the false gods will kill him.

And the Lord said unto him, Therefore whosoever slayeth Cain, vengeance shall be taken on him sevenfold. And the Lord set a mark upon Cain, lest any finding him should kill him.

–Genesis 4:15

The Lord was probably talking to, or at least within earshot of, Lucifer and the fallen gods. The mark was obviously a spiritual mark; perhaps denoting Cain was from the Lord.

And Cain went out from the presence of the Lord, and dwelt in the land of Nod, on the east of Eden.

–Genesis 4:16

Judgment comes upon Cain, who can no longer even till the ground and will have to live in the earth, probably in caves. He will depend on others to survive.

Because the ground is now cursed and cannot even grow herbs, we can speculate this is when animal meat became a chosen food source for Cain and the wholesale slaughter of earth animals began.

Cain is desperate because he thinks someone will kill him for causing the cursed ground on the earth. The false gods know he is from the Lord and is perhaps the one who will defeat Lucifer, their leader.

But the Lord gives Cain a spiritual mark, showing whoever kills Cain will receive seven times the vengeance from the Lord.

Cain leaves Eden, away from God, and moves to a place called Nod, which was east of Eden. How was there a land called Nod if it wasn't already in existence, and somebody outside of Eden to name the land of Nod?

This is more evidence of the fallen angels Cain was afraid of and who were destroying the earth, existed outside the kingdom of God and Eden.

When We Lived East of Eden

And Cain knew his wife; and she conceived, and bare Enoch: and he builded a city, and called the name of the city, after the name of his son, Enoch.

–Genesis 4:17

According to most Bible teachers, Cain is believed to have married his sister. However, it doesn't say his sister. It also takes more than one person to build a city—many more.

Centuries could have passed before he found a wife, or he might have married a woman long down Seth's lineage. She could also be a progeny of the fallen gods. There were probably women as fallen beings as well. It doesn't mean he had to marry his sister.

Then lifted I up mine eyes, and looked, and, behold, there came out two women, and the wind was in their wings; for they had wings like the wings of a stork: and they lifted up the ephah between the earth and the heaven.

–Zechariah 5:9

In the vision to Zechariah, there were spiritual women, not angels, but separate beings as women. Cain could have married one of these fallen female beings.

If it mattered, God would have put it in His Word. It just shows the start of the Cain lineage.

His descendants learned from the false gods how to make things and survive.

Were our spirits part of this lineage? It makes sense this is when we spiritually existed east of Eden in our fallen spirit bodies.

Lord, thou hast been our dwelling place in all generations.

Before the mountains were brought forth, or ever thou hadst formed the earth and the world, even from everlasting to everlasting, thou art God.

Thou turnest man to destruction; and sayest, Return, ye children of men.

–Psalm 90:1-3

These are more verses that show we existed with God before He moved us out of the spiritual earth's destruction into our current universe and earth.

Educators taught us that ancient people were stupid cave dwellers, but it wasn't the case. We were intelligent spirits, learning from the false gods. When we read Genesis chapter 4, we could build cities and pagan towers for worship, raise animals, make musical instruments, and construct brass and iron into weapons and other items as needed. Archaeologists have discovered ancient-type batteries, computers, and other technological instruments.

Our minds wire us to a particular vocation on our planet, but we don't know why. We do if we can now see our eternal soul instructing us from when we were doing a similar occupation east of Eden, under the rule of the false gods.

It also explains why pagan souls, going back to Nimrod, crafted and worshiped idols made in the likeness of animals or gods—to worship the false gods east of Eden who came from the spirit realm.

One thing to note in the Cain lineage is it only describes mostly singular offspring. This implies the false gods impregnated at least some women, which we will see later produced giants. Overall, they still could have produced billions of people over the ages.

Also, after Cain, the term 'knew' is no longer used. It changes to begat from the men. It shows the uniqueness of Cain's seed lineage. His descendants begat under the false gods, and we will see how Adam begat under God.

It seems one of Cain's descendants, Lamech, killed Cain, who was still a young man after passing centuries.

Despite Cain's deception from Lucifer, he was still a "knew" from the Lord. It is apparent, the false gods convinced Lamech to kill him. This was one more cause for the flood, to remove the earth and evil beings out of His world.

And Lamech said unto his wives, Adah and Zillah, Hear my voice; ye wives of Lamech, hearken unto my speech: for I have slain a man to my wounding, and a young man to my hurt.

If Cain shall be avenged sevenfold, truly Lamech seventy and sevenfold.

–Genesis 4:23-24

Cain's lineage in this chapter, so far, doesn't show how long they lived, as it does for Adam's descendants. It is because they were destroyed in the flood, whereas Adam's line, except for Noah and his family, died before the flood.

The rebellion against God is growing on the spiritual earth. Just as the rebellion against God is growing now on our planet. The devil has deceived our world, just as he did in heaven. What is good is now bad, and what is bad is now good. Is our moral compass from God broken?

How did we get so immorally bamboozled? Can we not see how eternal darkness is coming on the horizon? Wake up!

God Begins the
Restoration of Man

And Adam knew his wife again; and she bare a son, and called his name Seth: For God, said she, hath appointed me another seed instead of Abel, whom Cain slew.

And to Seth, to him also there was born a son; and he called his name Enos: then began men to call upon the name of the Lord.

–Genesis 4:25-26

Eve is still sorrowful and, again, does not acknowledge Adam having the seed of the living soul to produce Seth. This time she says God, instead of the Lord, gave her Seth, because Genesis chapter 5 will restore the Adam lineage to God. She believes Seth is a distinct descendant of God, destined to replace Cain and Abel, and bruise the head of evil.

However, Seth was the spiritual patriarchal beginning of the lineage that would eventually bring Yeshua or Jesus to our earth.

Seth's descendants apparently live in Eden with the Lord, while Cain's is in the destructed earth, ground, with the false gods.

Seth has a son named Enos. Interestingly, Seth's wife and future wives' names are missing. The last verse, "then began men to call upon the Lord," shows us the reason—they repented. Because of this, God can start restoring Adam's lineage into His kingdom so they can continue restoring his earth. He will restore them as male-female.

For whosoever shall call upon the name of the Lord shall be saved.

–Romans 10:13

The rest of the lineage is described as begat from the men. This is further evidence the Lord God had some input in the birthing of Cain, Abel, and Seth, or why the term "knew" and later begat are used.

Eve had previously said she got the man from the Lord. It was different for Seth, though, because God is now in the picture to restore the lineage from Adam. This time, she claims Seth is from God.

The last verse, calling on the name of the Lord, is critical to helping us put the creation story together. Adam, Eve, Seth, and his descendants get restored to God's kingdom. Why? Because the men began to call upon the name of the Lord.

The following scriptures support the Genesis chapter 1 restoration.

From Genesis, chapter 5:

This is the book of the generations of Adam. In the day that God created man, in the likeness of God made he him;

Male and female created he them; and blessed them, and called their name Adam, in the day when they were created.

–Genesis 5: 1-2

Do these verses sound familiar? They are from the Lord God, drawing our attention back to Genesis 1, when God restores man to His kingdom. Adam's spiritual descendants, now begat as unique from God, are restored or born-again in God's kingdom in the likeness of God.

After they died, their souls were probably brought into God's kingdom through the gate or portal guarded by the cherubs and flaming sword in the Garden.

And Jacob awaked out of his sleep, and he said, Surely the LORD is in this place; and I knew *it* not. And he was afraid, and said, How dreadful *is* this place! this *is* none other but the house of God, and this *is* the gate of heaven.

–Genesis 28:16-17

Dreadful could have been translated as awesome. Jacob had seen a ladder or staircase going into heaven with a gate. This is how we will enter the kingdom of God if Jesus has saved us.

He that overcometh, the same shall be clothed in white raiment; and I will not blot out his name out of the book of life, but I will confess his name before my Father, and before his angels.

–Revelation 3:5

God is telling us how Adam's family were the first to be in His book of life.

There are several important items to emphasize here and in this chapter.

The narrative changes back to God and Genesis 1, where God made and then created man in His image and likeness. We saw the restoration process for man start when he began to call upon the name of the Lord.

This is a new generation in God's kingdom, the restored male-female mentioned in Genesis 1:26-27, starting with Adam.

Thus, God creates from the Lord's made man, Adam, in His image and likeness. He also combines Adam and Eve as one in God, calling him the first male-female Adam.

And Adam lived an hundred and thirty years, and begat a son in his own likeness, and after his image; and called his name Seth:

–Genesis 5:1-3

The next thing to note is the term "knew" changes to "begat". It doesn't say Adam "knew" Seth into existence, but that Adam begat

Seth. Adam now has the likeness and image of God, and he begets Seth from God.

When God restores us to His kingdom through Jesus, we are one male-female. This unity will now begat offspring in the kingdom of God.

The Lord uses begat to show the difference now or the uniqueness of Adam's line in God's kingdom. Cain's line of begat shows the uniqueness of not being in God's kingdom.

The chapter reveals how long Adam's genealogy lived until they died and how God's realm quickly filled with those to bring new life into His realm after they died before the flood. They still suffered the consequences of Adam's sin and death, yet lived as restored in God's kingdom. We can do the same today.

The last of Cain's descendants lived for 120 years, and God destroyed them in the flood of our earth. They-we now need Jesus to return to God's kingdom.

It shows us Cain, and his descendants are not part of God restoring them into his kingdom. They are under and worshiping the false gods outside of Eden.

When the flood comes to remove Cain's descendants with their animals, their false gods, and the destroyed "without form and void" earth into our physical realm, Seth's lineage will be or are restored into God's kingdom. There is no need for them to be born on our earth.

As we saw when David cried out to God during the flood, although his spirit probably wasn't one of the patriarchs, he was seemingly from Cain's descendants. However, because he cried out to God, His spirit soul was in heaven while being born and going through life on our earth.

The same is probably true for us, if our souls cried out to God during the flood, and who accept God's eternal plan of salvation through Jesus during our physical lives.

And the days of Adam after he had begotten Seth were eight hundred years: and he begat sons and daughters:

And all the days that Adam lived were nine hundred and thirty years: and he died.

And Seth lived an hundred and five years, and begat Enos:

And Seth lived after he begat Enos eight hundred and seven years, and begat sons and daughters:

And all the days of Seth were nine hundred and twelve years: and he died.

And Enos lived ninety years, and begat Cainan:

And Enos lived after he begat Cainan eight hundred and fifteen years, and begat sons and daughters:

And all the days of Enos were nine hundred and five years: and he died.

And Cainan lived seventy years and begat Mahalaleel:

And Cainan lived after he begat Mahalaleel eight hundred and forty years, and begat sons and daughters:

And all the days of Cainan were nine hundred and ten years: and he died.

And Mahalaleel lived sixty and five years, and begat Jared:

And Mahalaleel lived after he begat Jared eight hundred and thirty years, and begat sons and daughters:

And all the days of Mahalaleel were eight hundred ninety and five years: and he died.

And Enoch walked with God after he begat Methuselah three hundred years, and begat sons and daughters:

And all the days of Enoch were three hundred sixty and five years:

And Enoch walked with God: and he was not; for God took him.

And Methuselah lived an hundred eighty and seven years, and begat Lamech.

And Methuselah lived after he begat Lamech seven hundred eighty and two years, and begat sons and daughters:

And all the days of Methuselah were nine hundred sixty and nine years: and he died.

And Lamech lived an hundred eighty and two years, and begat a son:

And he called his name Noah, saying, This same shall comfort us concerning our work and toil of our hands, because of the ground which the Lord hath cursed.

And Lamech lived after he begat Noah five hundred ninety and five years, and begat sons and daughters:

And all the days of Lamech were seven hundred seventy and seven years: and he died.

And Noah was five hundred years old: and Noah begat Shem, Ham, and Japheth.

–Genesis 5:4-32

Please reread Genesis chapters 4 and 5 to contrast the differences between the Cain and Seth lines of descendants.

We entered the Adam descendants to get us to Enoch and show another reason God brought in the flood.

It says God took Enoch as he walked with God. Possibly, he was the last of the Seth descendants living in Eden, and Methuselah and Lamech, with Noah, moved to the earth's ground.

The latter portions of these scriptures mention the cursed ground again. After Enoch, the rest of the descendants were on the cursed ground, and Noah somehow comforted their lives on the cursed ground of the earth. It seems the curse was removed before transcending into our earth, so we could survive until our resurrection.

With Noah, they were still the descendants of Adam's line, and they begat souls, male and female, into God's kingdom. However, something bad is about to happen since the descendants of Enoch left Eden and the Lord's protection.

Here Comes the Judge

And it came to pass, when men began to multiply on the face of the earth, and daughters were born unto them,

That the sons of God saw the daughters of men that they were fair; and they took them wives of all which they chose.

And the Lord said, My spirit shall not always strive with man, for that he also is flesh: yet his days shall be an hundred and twenty years.

–Genesis 6:1-3

If we follow the logic of the story, the men mentioned in the first verse, with sons and daughters, were probably from Methuselah and Lemech. As they came from Eden, their daughters were fair and became targets for the false gods to corrupt.

We now see that Cain's descendants died after a hundred and twenty years because of the inbreeding with the fallen gods.

It also compares the spirit of the Lord with man, as flesh or spirit, confirming we were all spirit bodies before the Lord birthed us on our earth.

There are a few things to note here in the final chapters.

1. The narrative switches back and forth between God and the Lord.

2. The creation story now moves the perspective out of Eden again, investigating the affairs of the fallen beings on the face of the earth.

There is the earth, the face of the earth, and in the earth, along with the ground.

This is loosely divided into the world as Eden on earth—affixed to God's kingdom through the Garden. The face of the earth—where the fallen gods were. In the earth—where Cain's descendants lived in caves—and the ground, or the general area outside of Eden. Admittedly, it doesn't always jump out at us what the difference is.

However, the verses show us when God speaks; He talks with Noah's restored soul, who will end up on the restored earth after the flood. The physical soul of Noah travels to our earth.

Genesis, chapter 6, proves there were false gods on the face of the earth, not in Eden. Only after many daughters came from Methuselah and Lamech did the false gods take those daughters and have offspring with them.

They were fair because they were from Eden, and the gods wanted to corrupt them to spite the Lord and disrupt the line to Jesus. They didn't know the line to Jesus would be through Noah and his descendants.

There was something special about these daughters from Adam's lineage mixed with the false gods: they produced giants or mighty men.

It also infers the women from Cain's line were not as fair as those from Eden, because many were probably the progeny of fallen women.

There were giants in the earth in those days; and also after that, when the sons of God came in unto the daughters of men, and they bare children to them, the same became mighty men which were of old, men of renown.

And God saw that the wickedness of man was great in the earth, and that every imagination of the thoughts of his heart was only evil continually.

And it repented the Lord that he had made man on the earth, and it grieved him at his heart.

–Genesis 6: 4-6

The giants refer to the descendants of fallen gods, and the sons of God were perhaps different fallen beings, describing the name of the fallen gods and stealing the daughters from Eden.

It is probable these evil offspring would later produce the evil leaders of our history and current time, all acting as false gods.

Things have to be or get pretty bad for the Lord to grieve and repent.

To recall what has happened so far:

1.   Lucifer deceived Adam and Eve and caused a separation between man and the Lord.

2.   Lucifer also deceived Cain, causing him to suffer and be separated from the Lord.

3.   Cain probably started the killing of animals for food since he caused the ground to be cursed and not provide food.

4.   Lamech killed Cain, who was a "knew" from the Lord.

5.   The sons of God were stealing and corrupting the daughters from Eden and from, essentially, God.

It was the final straw.

Before Adam and Genesis 1, God had created all spirit beings and angels. The false gods were not literal sons of God, as only Jesus was the son of God. However, they are called the sons of God, which we call false gods, worded as such to separate them from Cain's descendants, who were also corrupting the earth.

So, on top of everything else, God lost Lucifer, trillions of angels, and probably the same amount of other fallen beings.

Want to get an idea of how many? Just look out at our universe, with all the fallen stars and planets held within the nations of galaxies. The universe represents the destructed spiritual earth and all the causalities from God's Genesis beginning. They are held in judgment until the end.

We only have glimpses from the Bible of the created beings in God's world. We know of cherubs, seraphs, angels, watchers, and women with wings.

People usually associate Lucifer-Satan as an angel, but he wasn't. He was first a cherub, closest to God.

After his rebellion, it appears he became a seraph, which has a description of a dragon, before he fell to earth and the Lord judged him as a worm.

Above him stood the seraphim. Each had six wings: with two he covered his face, and with two he covered his feet, and with two he flew.

–Isaiah 6:2

God looks down upon His destructed earth with His new council of old and restored beings and sees everyone is corrupt.

The Lord repents for what the inhabitants and earth have become, or corrupted as it is without form and void, like a wasteland.

And the Lord said, I will destroy man whom I have created from the face of the earth; both man, and beast, and the creeping thing, and the fowls of the air; for it repenteth me that I have made them.

–Genesis 6:7

This verse shows us the Lord "will destroy man whom I have created." Yet, we know the Lord formed or made man, as stated in the last verse.

It is speaking of what has happened to man and created-restored man. Adam's descendants, now created as restored, all died as destroyed before the flood, except for Noah and his family. Cain's and the false gods' descendants, still living along with the false gods, died in the flood.

For then must he often have suffered since the foundation of the world: but now once in the end of the world hath he appeared to put away sin by the sacrifice of himself.

And as it is appointed unto men once to die, but after this the judgment:

So Christ was once offered to bear the sins of many; and unto them that look for him shall he appear the second time without sin unto salvation.

–Hebrews 9:26-28

The end of our current world hasn't ended yet, so these verses are referring to the foundation and the end of His earth. His sacrifice of repentance was a death unto himself. Just as when we repent, it is death unto ourselves. Jesus physically carried out the death of our sins in our physical realm, just as we carry out our death to ourselves when we repent in our realm.

For if we have been planted together in the likeness of his death, we shall be also in the likeness of his resurrection:

Knowing this, that our old man is crucified with him, that the body of sin might be destroyed, that henceforth we should not serve sin.

For he that is dead is freed from sin.

–Romans 6:7-7

Jesus took on our sins; He became our sins; He was crucified for our sins. It was the only way sin could die, and we could be resurrected and restored in His likeness, as Adam's descendants were.

Everything was utterly evil on His earth, and Jesus removed all sin out of the sight of God in the spirit realm into our universe and world.

The animals became evil after Cain's descendants, and the beasts avenged their kind. The beasts no longer ate the grass and herbs from the field, but dined on Cain's descendants.

We are now seeing more animals attacking people on our planet because we are destroying their habitat and moving into their territories.

Continuing:

But Noah found grace in the eyes of the Lord.

These are the generations of Noah: Noah was a just man and perfect in his generations, and Noah walked with God.

And Noah begat three sons, Shem, Ham, and Japheth.

The earth also was corrupt before God, and the earth was filled with violence.

And God looked upon the earth, and, behold, it was corrupt; for all flesh had corrupted his way upon the earth.

And God said unto Noah, The end of all flesh is come before me; for the earth is filled with violence through them; and, behold, I will destroy them with the earth.

–Genesis 6:8-13

It says Noah walked with God, just as Enoch did, which means God restored his spirit and soul along with his family. God confirms with the Lord that all is lost. He says all flesh or spirit beings on earth are corrupt. It includes the false or sons of God with their fallen women, man and woman, the land, and animals.

The false gods must have done something to the earth, as it was apparently coming apart at the seams, filled with violence. Were there nuclear-type bombs exploding? Will this be the start of our universal demise?

God will turn the without form and void earth and dark waters from Genesis 1 into a flood and take Eden with it. The entrance through the Garden in Eden to God's restored kingdom is now removed for anyone else on earth. It will take a spiritual ark during the flood to get to heaven.

To the end that none of all the trees by the waters exalt themselves for their height, neither shoot up their top among the thick boughs, neither their trees stand up in their height, all that drink water: for they are all delivered unto death, to the nether parts of the earth, in the midst of the children of men, with them that go down to the pit.

–Ezekiel 31:14

Eden was governed by the Lord God and given to Adam's descendants. The false gods had jurisdiction over the ground surrounding Eden—just as today, Israel is God's land, given to the Jewish people by Seth's descendants, surrounded by nations governed by false gods.

For we wrestle not against flesh and blood, but against principalities, against powers, against the rulers of the darkness of this world, against spiritual wickedness in high places.

–Ephesians 6:12

Our universe-earth will be destroyed again, not by water but by fire.

But the heavens and the earth, which are now, by the same word are kept in store, reserved unto fire against the day of judgment and perdition of ungodly men.

–2nd Peter 3:7

Just as the ungodly men deceived by the false gods destroyed the earth before the flood, the same will destroy our earth. Lucifer, his spirit name, is Satan's physical name, and we are destroying our earth, environment, animals, food, and ourselves, as we did with God's earth.

Our earth will destroy the ungodly once again, except this time in fire, perhaps started by nuclear weapons. Thankfully, God has restored His world for all those who use the keys of the kingdom to return there.

Preparing For The Flood

And God said unto Noah, The end of all flesh is come before me; for the earth is filled with violence through them; and, behold, I will destroy them with the earth.

Make thee an ark of gopher wood; rooms shalt thou make in the ark, and shalt pitch it within and without with pitch.

And this is the fashion which thou shalt make it of: The length of the ark shall be three hundred cubits, the breadth of it fifty cubits, and the height of it thirty cubits.

A window shalt thou make to the ark, and in a cubit shalt thou finish it above; and the door of the ark shalt thou set in the side thereof; with lower, second, and third stories shalt thou make it.

–Genesis 6:13

The narrative of the flood starts with God. It is interesting to note, Noah didn't ask God what an ark was but just heard what to make it out of and how big to make it. He walked with God and was therefore in spiritual communion and knowledge with Him.

A cubit is the measurement between a man's elbow and his middle finger. Surprisingly, it is accurate to eighteen inches. Sometimes, it included a span, which was added onto the cubit, or about six inches. From this, we can judge that the ark was 450 feet long, 75 feet wide, and 45 feet high, according to our physical measurements.

If it was a spiritual measurement, it may have been much larger. This is still similar in style to the ocean tankers in our modern world.

And, behold, I, even I, do bring a flood of waters upon the earth, to destroy all flesh, wherein is the breath of life, from under heaven; and every thing that is in the earth shall die.

But with thee will I establish my covenant; and thou shalt come into the ark, thou, and thy sons, and thy wife, and thy sons' wives with thee.

And of every living thing of all flesh, two of every sort shalt thou bring into the ark, to keep them alive with thee; they shall be male and female.

Of fowls after their kind, and of cattle after their kind, of every creeping thing of the earth after his kind, two of every sort shall come unto thee, to keep them alive.

And take thou unto thee of all food that is eaten, and thou shalt gather it to thee; and it shall be for food for thee, and for them.

Thus did Noah; according to all that God commanded him, so did he.

–Genesis 6:13-22

This is the first separation of the spiritual flesh of Noah and animals when God communicates to the spirit of Noah to build an ark because God will destroy the earth.

The spirit or flesh of Noah, his family, and wives will bring two of every animal flesh into His kingdom. It implies Noah is bringing the animals and food from Eden, as it was probably the only place that still had clean animals and edible food.

Remember, the Lord made this earth, so it appears God is taking jurisdiction here, at least concerning Noah's spirit, and destroying all flesh that has the breath of life from under heaven. God and the Lord agree this has to happen: "I, even I, do bring a flood upon the earth."

The main thought we might take from this is God tells Noah to take these animals from Eden. This is apparent because there wasn't a lot of good food available, even if the Lord removed part of the cursed ground for Noah. This meant the animals in Eden still had food and were considered clean.

Therefore, what is implied is there were two arks: a spiritual ark to bring the flesh of Noah, his family, and animals to God's kingdom, and a physical ark to bring Noah, his family, and animals from the land outside of Eden to our earth.

We can't imagine the power and force it took to separate and move the destroyed earth out of His realm to form our realm. It shook heaven and earth.

The spiritual ark would keep the animals from Eden safe, two male and female. All this ark had to do was float up to heaven, protect the inhabitants of every living creature, and provide enough food for them to eat. These animals from Eden were raised into God's kingdom as part of the Genesis 1 restoration.

When the vision of God's kingdom opened so certain men or prophets could see into it, they would see the firmament, the bow or rainbow, and the Ark of the Covenant. Would it be any more different to see the spiritual ark also?

Next, the Lord shows us His flood version, or when our physical realm came into existence.

The Lord's Flood

We just saw the spiritual flood image from God. Next, we are shown the flood from the Lord.

We've explained a portion of the details from God. Now, we will back up and get a better overview of the earth's destruction and flood(s) in the spirit realm, reflecting Genesis 1:2.

Most people skim over the details of Noah's flood, as it seems the story repeats itself. And, of course, the bamboozled religious teachers didn't help us.

Thus, we learned from these Bible teachers how God flooded our earth but kept Noah, his family, and two of each kind of animal, male and female, alive in a vast boat. It also says Noah brought clean animals. It rains for 40 days and nights, ignoring the first seven days. The ark finally came to rest on Mt. Ararat, and everyone and the animals departed to fill our earth.

However, we will see far more to the story than what we've learned yesteryear. The flood from God's world became our universe, and yes, our earth experienced a global flood, but it isn't the essence of the story.

To begin with, God, the Lord, and the Spirit of God play a part in the flood story. God commands the destruction of the fallen earth, and the Lord affirms His commands, "I even I".

God chooses Noah and his family, or their souls are reserved for the restored earth. However, during the transition, they also become physical beings, so they can survive on our planet as they transfer into our universe.

It appears souls are one, yet they can be separated and connected with a spiritual string of consciousness. Later, we will have two souls in God's kingdom again when we are combined as male-female.

It would be like when the Lord separated the woman from Adam, and Eve became a living female soul through Adam's soul.

It didn't say she became a living soul, but she had to be in order to exist. Adam, originally, had to have two souls, male and female, and the female soul became the woman after God removed the rib or womb from Adam.

The living soul of man transfers a new soul from God into the woman to form a child, and they are connected spiritually. The male-female souls are reunited into one when restored in God's kingdom.

God, inclusive with the Lord, determines the spiritual earth has become forever corrupt and lost. It is the equivalent of dark waters or a sea—a place to dump the remnants of a sin-filled world of false gods, corrupted souls, and animals. The only way to rid it all out of His world is to convert the darkened sea into another realm. It is time to transport the without-form and void spiritual earth into a physical realm.

First, God told Noah to build the ark and bring in two of every kind of animal, male and female.

The Lord adds to this, bringing in clean beasts and fowl by sevens. What denotes a clean animal? The Bible consistently shows the number seven determines completeness or wholeness. The clean animals come from Eden. This means the Lord told Noah to bring clean animals by sevens from Eden with unclean animals from the earth into the ark. Otherwise, there wouldn't be a designation for clean animals.

Then, there are iterations of the flood and loading the ark.

When the flood came, it says it rained for forty days and forty nights, which is the first mention of night since Genesis 1. This means the physical realm and earth are now formed, and the flood covered the mountains. Yet, the flood rose 15 cubits, or about 22½ feet, to cover the hills. They were not very high mountains, or the flood only rose high enough to cover anyone or anything standing on a mountain.

The flood continues, removing the without-form and void earth into our current universe and world, with the physical ark in transit.

Admittedly, the old flood story seems jumbled until we bring in God and the Lord and recognize the two different perspectives.

People have difficulty understanding God, especially with our finite minds. We can somewhat explain it in this manner.

Arguably, the founding fathers used principles from the Bible to establish the United States. The Constitution created three government sections, including the legislative, executive, and judicial branches. Each has its own functions and boundaries.

Congress, also known as the legislative branch, creates laws. The executive branch, or the President, signs these laws and directs their execution. The judicial branch, or judges, ensures none of the laws created are unconstitutional or that the other two branches haven't overstepped their bounds. Unfortunately, through being bamboozled by not learning from history, we are quickly falling away from our original concept of a constitutional government.

Yet, the three separate entities—legislative, executive, and judicial—function as one government. This is similar to how the Father, Son, and Holy Spirit operate and interact as one God, and we can see it concerning the flood.

We know God oversaw the restoration in Genesis 1 and is now with the Lord to deal with the fallen earth. During the restoration, God saw what was happening in the fallen world and was determined to remove it from His world, and the Lord did so as a flood.

And the Lord said unto Noah, Come thou and all thy house into the ark; for thee have I seen righteous before me in this generation.

Of every clean beast thou shalt take to thee by sevens, the male and his female: and of beasts that are not clean by two, the male and his female.

Of fowls also of the air by sevens, the male and the female; to keep seed alive upon the face of all the earth.

–Genesis 7:1-3

These verses differ from what God told restored Noah. God said to bring in all animals in twos, male and female. Here, the Lord adds clean beasts by sevens and fowls by sevens, which will keep seed alive or spread them throughout our earth, since there won't be any plants or trees left after the flood on our earth.

Now, this physical Noah has clean and unclean beasts and fowl, along with two's of every male and female animal. We will soon see why this Noah brought clean beasts and fowl to our planet.

The beasts are the highest order of animals, so they can mutate into the lower or different species we see today. However, they were probably the infants of beasts and fowl to fit on the ark and who would be easier to care for, not eat a lot of food, and have enough time on our earth to replicate many times in their lifespan.

For yet seven days, and I will cause it to rain upon the earth forty days and forty nights; and every living substance that I have made will I destroy from off the face of the earth.

And Noah did according unto all that the Lord commanded him.

And Noah was six hundred years old when the flood of waters was upon the earth.

And Noah went in, and his sons, and his wife, and his sons' wives with him, into the ark, because of the waters of the flood.

Of clean beasts, and of beasts that are not clean, and of fowls, and of every thing that creepeth upon the earth,

–Genesis 7:4-8

This is the first flood, which will commence in seven days. Why seven days? Because it is also showing the start of God restoring His earth in Genesis 1, along with the Lord's formation of our physical realm in seven days from a without form and void spiritual earth.

Noah did all that the Lord had commanded him with the clean and unclean animals, and they went into the ark "because of the waters of the flood." This is part of the first rendition. But in the next verse, it starts over.

There went in two and two unto Noah into the ark, the male and the female, as God had commanded Noah.

–Genesis 7:9

It jumps back to Genesis chapter 6, where God told Noah to bring in two of every kind but doesn't mention or separate the clean animals because they are all clean from Eden and going to God's kingdom.

We saw the physical Noah loading the animals for our earth; at the same time, the spirit Noah is loading the spirit ark for God.

Thus, there were two commandments: one from God to bring in the male and female animals from Eden, and one from the Lord to bring in the unclean animals from the earth and the clean sevens from Eden. The physical and spiritual Noah obeyed both the Lord and God.

Noah, with the clean and unclean animals, are already in the ark because of the flood, when God tells the spirit Noah to bring in the male and female, not mentioning clean animals.

There had to be two arks, and it cannot be happening on our earth!

And it came to pass after seven days, that the waters of the flood were upon the earth.

In the six hundredth year of Noah's life, in the second month, the seventeenth day of the month, the same day were all the fountains of the great deep broken up, and the windows of heaven were opened.

And the rain was upon the earth forty days and forty nights.

–Genesis 7:10-12

These verses continue as Noah, with both clean and unclean animals, are flooded into the physical realm: "… the fountains of the great deep broken up, and the windows of heaven were opened." It says the windows of heaven opened, not the sky. Were the fountains of the great deep and the windows of heaven the black holes in our universe spewing out the making of our universe?

However, the description starts over again.

In the selfsame day entered Noah, and Shem, and Ham, and Japheth, the sons of Noah, and Noah's wife, and the three wives of his sons with them, into the ark;

They, and every beast after his kind, and all the cattle after their kind, and every creeping thing that creepeth upon the earth after his kind, and every fowl after his kind, every bird of every sort.

And they went in unto Noah into the ark, two and two of all flesh, wherein is the breath of life.

And they that went in, went in male and female of all flesh, as God had commanded him: and the Lord shut him in.

–Genesis 7:13-16

The flood already happened, yet this verse says in the same day, Noah is loading the ark again. There is no addition of clean animals in this ark because they are all clean from Eden, going to the kingdom of God.

We saw how Noah and the ark were already in the physical realm. These verses convey the restored Noah with all the spirit or flesh animals in two's from Eden going into God's restored earth.

These flood events involved two aspects of God: and the Lord, with Noah obeying each, and who couldn't possibly perform two of the same commandments at the same time on our planet.

We need to see two events happen simultaneously. One description transfers Noah and his family in the ark into the physical realm—"the same day were all the fountains of the great deep broken up, and the windows of heaven were opened."

The windows of heaven opened to establish our physical realm, to bring our universe and earth into existence, and to shuttle the ark into the great deep of our universe to our now-formed planet.

The second description in the "self-same day" is of the spiritually restored Noah and his family, with the animals transferring into the restored kingdom of God.

In the second description, we find the ark floating above the earth. This is when it entered the kingdom of God on Mount Zion. It doesn't say this, but remember the binary effects. What happens on our earth already happened in heaven.

And the flood was forty days upon the earth; and the waters increased, and bare up the ark, and it was lift up above the earth.

And the waters prevailed, and were increased upon the earth; and the ark went upon the face of the waters.

And the waters prevailed exceedingly upon the earth; and all the high hills, that were under the whole heaven, were covered.

Fifteen cubits upward did the waters prevail; and the mountains were covered.

And all flesh died that moved upon the earth, both of fowl, and of cattle, and of beast, and of every creeping thing that creepeth upon the earth, and every man:

All in whose nostrils was the breath of life, of all that was in the dry land, died.

And every living substance was destroyed which was upon the face of the ground, both man, and cattle, and the creeping things, and the fowl of the heaven; and they were destroyed from the earth: and Noah only remained alive, and they that were with him in the ark.

And the waters prevailed upon the earth an hundred and fifty days.

–Genesis 7:17-24

These verses state all flesh, as spiritual beings, died who were left over on the face of the ground. Once the arks departed, with the physical side of Noah, his family, and animals riding the earth, flooding into the physical realm—the restored Noah, his family and animals were raised to heaven.

The flood did its job and destroyed everything left on the ground, and flushed into our universe.

The spiritual ark lifted above the earth until waters were under the whole heaven to transport the spirit ark into God's kingdom.

We know nothing created from God can be completely destroyed, but they changed into physical elements in our universe and earth, or as restored in God's kingdom..

The Separated Worlds

Finally, we see the flood end on God's earth, or when the firmament passed through in Genesis 1:7, separating the waters under and above the firmament. The following narrative is about God and Noah on the restored earth.

And God remembered Noah, and every living thing, and all the cattle that was with him in the ark: and God made a wind to pass over the earth, and the waters assuaged;

–Genesis 8:1

The dark waters, or darkness, are gone from His original earth. The Eden animals and Noah's family can now safely leave the ark in heaven. The next verse is when God finishes our universe, and He shows the physical ark on our earth or the waters under the firmament.

The fountains also of the deep and the windows of heaven were stopped, and the rain from heaven was restrained;

And the waters returned from off the earth continually: and after the end of the hundred and fifty days the waters were abated.

And the ark rested in the seventh month, on the seventeenth day of the month, upon the mountains of Ararat.

–Genesis 8:2-4

And it came to pass at the end of forty days, that Noah opened the window of the ark which he had made:

And he sent forth a raven, which went forth to and fro, until the waters were dried up from off the earth.

Also, he sent forth a dove from him, to see if the waters were abated from off the face of the ground; But the dove found no rest for the sole of her foot, and she returned unto him into the ark, for the waters were on the face of the whole earth: then he put forth his hand, and took her, and pulled her in unto him into the ark.

–Genesis 8:5-9

After only 40 days, the mountain tops showed. Noah must have seen the earth was still flooded, so why send out birds? They are symbolic.

The dark waters of our universe and earth still haven't dried up, for the raven symbolizes evil, which still goes to and fro around our earth until the end.

If the raven was flying around without stopping, why send out a dove too?

Because it is different worlds, and the dove is the Spirit of God, showing us the restoration process is starting from Genesis 1:3.

And he stayed yet other seven days; and again he sent forth the dove out of the ark; And the dove came in to him in the evening; and, lo, in her mouth was an olive leaf pluckt off: so Noah knew that the waters were abated from off the earth. And he stayed yet other seven days; and sent forth the dove; which returned not again unto him any more.

–Genesis 8:10-12

This is when the Spirit of God started restoring His earth, and the dove could show the spirit Noah with the olive leaf. This leaf also symbolized peace with God toward man.

After seven days, Genesis 1 ended, so the dove, or Spirit of God, did not return to Noah. The 'dove' is symbolized again when he returns to our earth, when Jesus came.

And Jesus, when he was baptized, went up straightway out of the water: and, lo, the heavens were opened unto him, and he saw the Spirit of God descending like a dove, and lighting upon him:

–Matthew 3:16

Starting with Genesis chapter 8:20, the story's narrative turns back to the Lord and Noah on our earth.

And Noah builded an altar unto the Lord; and took of every clean beast, and of every clean fowl, and offered burnt offerings on the altar.

And the Lord smelled a sweet savour; and the Lord said in his heart, I will not again curse the ground any more for man's sake; for the imagination of man's heart is evil from his youth;

neither will I again smite any more every thing living, as I have done.

While the earth remaineth, seedtime and harvest, and cold and heat, and summer and winter, and day and night shall not cease.

–Genesis 8:20-22

Now we know why the Lord gave Noah clean animals—to take as a sacrifice for our corrupted earth. It removed the rest of the curse from our earth so all things could grow and thrive again.

In these last Genesis chapter verses, we see how the Lord has removed the curse from the land so people can eat food other than weeds. The fowl will spread new seeds throughout the earth to grow produce and orchards of every kind.

Not only will Noah's descendants, down through the ages, provide the heel, as the Jewish descendants, to wound Satan's head to the coming Savior, but the clean animals will also provide for the Jewish people to sacrifice and consume to cover their sins.

But I have said unto you, Ye shall inherit their land, and I will give it unto you to possess it, a land that floweth with milk and honey: I am the Lord your God, which have separated you from other people.

Ye shall therefore put difference between clean beasts and unclean, and between unclean fowls and clean: and ye shall not make your souls abominable by beast, or by fowl, or by any manner of living thing that creepeth on the ground, which I have separated from you as unclean.

And ye shall be holy unto me: for I the Lord am holy, and have severed you from other people, that ye should be mine.

–Leviticus 20:24-26

People are still controlled by the false gods of the devil, those who despise or want to destroy the Jewish population and Israel, the land God gave them, because the Lord God separated them as His own.

According to Bible prophecy, the time will come when the world will attack them in their country and try to destroy the Jews and Israel forever. This will happen just before the end of our time. (Ezekiel 38)

Life in Two Worlds

We have come to the end of the creation story. Genesis chapter 9 leaves us with God instructing Noah on the restored earth.

And God blessed Noah and his sons, and said unto them, Be fruitful, and multiply, and replenish the earth.

And the fear of you and the dread of you shall be upon every beast of the earth, and upon every fowl of the air, upon all that moveth upon the earth, and upon all the fishes of the sea; into your hand are they delivered.

–Genesis 9: 1-2

The first verse is the same message we saw in Genesis 1: towards restored man—be fruitful and multiply, replenish the earth, and have dominion over all the animals. The animals will know we have authority over them.

Every moving thing that liveth shall be meat for you; even as the green herb have I given you all things.

–Genesis 9:4

It means we will eat "every moving thing shall be meat" for us. It doesn't include animals, but plants, because it has green herbs in the context.

We will eat the food provided by the garden, and it will also supply us with herbs. We know herbs on our earth provide medicinal qualities and, therefore, will probably do the same in heaven.

All plants grow faster and constantly in heaven because there is no time; we will see them as moving, creeping things as they develop.

But flesh with the life thereof, which is the blood thereof, shall ye not eat.

And surely your blood of your lives will I require; at the hand of every beast will I require it, and at the hand of man; at the hand of every man's brother will I require the life of man.

Whoso sheddeth man's blood, by man shall his blood be shed: for in the image of God made he man.

–Genesis 9:4-6

It seems we will no longer eat meat or even have a desire to do so. These verses show we will not eat spirit meat as flesh. We will lose our current bloodthirstiness, where we now slaughter and consume billions of animals each year, just as we did in our destruction of the spiritual earth.

People say that when they quit eating meat, they can no longer stand the smell of it cooking, and it tastes disgusting. Through our deception of demonic bloodlust, we slaughter billions of creatures each year just to eat them.

Apparently, there will be some type of punishment if we eat an animal, and the life of man will somehow restore the animal. If we cause the life to be shed by another man, our life will restore the man.

God then turned or went to Noah on our earth and repeated the commandment to be fruitful and multiply.

And you, be ye fruitful, and multiply; bring forth abundantly in the earth, and multiply therein.

–Genesis 9:7

God makes a covenant with Noah that He won't destroy the restored earth with a flood and places the bow in His heaven.

The prophet Ezekiel saw it when he could view God's kingdom. The colors of the bow were all around the Lord.

As the appearance of the bow that is in the cloud in the day of rain, so was the appearance of the brightness round about. This was the appearance of the likeness of the glory of the Lord.

–Ezekiel 1:28

The creation story now ends, at least from God's perspective.

And God said, This is the token of the covenant which I make between me and you and every living creature that is with you, for perpetual generations:

I do set my bow in the cloud, and it shall be for a token of a covenant between me and the earth.

And it shall come to pass, when I bring a cloud over the earth, that the bow shall be seen in the cloud:

And I will remember my covenant, which is between me and you and every living creature of all flesh; and the waters shall no more become a flood to destroy all flesh.

And the bow shall be in the cloud; and I will look upon it, that I may remember the everlasting covenant between God and every living creature of all flesh that is upon the earth.

And God said unto Noah, This is the token of the covenant, which I have established between me and all flesh that is upon the earth.

–Genesis 9:12-17

God reaffirms his covenant with the spirit, Noah, because He is talking about all flesh. It states He will see the bow in the cloud, which we've assumed is our rainbow in our sky after it rains. It is, but this is referring to the bow in His heaven.

Probably, when we learned God said flesh is spirit, it made learning the difference between a spirit body and a physical body easier and helped resolve at least part of the mystery of creation.

This book is far from what religious teachers have taught us: the creation only concerns Genesis chapters 1 and perhaps 2.

It is apparent there will come persecution upon this book and the author as the bamboozled one. So be it. We need to hear the Spirit of God if we want to understand the Bible.

Whether we believe this story or the one handed down from centuries of religious deception, it doesn't matter. What matters is whether we are saved through Jesus' shed blood, using the kingdom tools He gave us. Repent, be baptized in His Spirit, follow Him, and His Holy Spirit will teach us all things.

By doing so, this book challenges readers to return to the Bible with a new outlook concerning what God has gone through so we can return to His kingdom.

The book has also shown us how we can understand the spiritual insight of the Bible once we see it through God's eyes and understanding instead of from a preconceived religious perspective. Ask God to reveal His wisdom to you.

He has given us the free will to determine our destiny. The prayer is everyone will choose the eternal light with God and not the eternal darkness with the devil and his minions.

Find out how many binary effects there are in this book, our lives, the environment, and the Bible. They are there to prove God is real, specifically for you!

This story will end with one last clarion call from God to us before the end of all things.

But if from thence thou shalt seek the Lord thy God, thou shalt find him, if thou seek him with all thy heart and with all thy soul.

When thou art in tribulation, and all these things are come upon thee, even in the latter days, if thou turn to the Lord thy God, and shalt be obedient unto his voice;

(For the Lord thy God is a merciful God;) he will not forsake thee, neither destroy thee, nor forget the covenant of thy fathers which he sware unto them.

For ask now of the days that are past, which were before thee, since the day that God created man upon the earth, and ask from the one side of heaven unto the other, whether there hath been any such thing as this great thing is, or hath been heard like it?

–Deuteronomy 4:29-32

Is there anything greater than God creating us on His restored earth? Ask Him, He is waiting for you to meet Him personally.

A p p e n d i x

Listed below on the left side are the Old Testament books in chronological order.

The books listed to the right with a dash are the books that took place at the same time for each particular book. In other words, the book of Job should be read with Genesis because it occurred during the creation events.

The dashed attached books could be skipped if one just wants to read the chronological order on the left side and then come back to see what they missed with the side books.

The supporting books of the prophets, and who they were attributed to, are at the end.

Genesis–Job

Exodus–Leviticus

Numbers–Deuteronomy

Joshua

Judges–Ruth

1st Samuel–1st Chronicles

2nd Samuel–1st Chronicles, Psalms

1st Kings–2nd Chronicles, Proverbs, Ecclesiastes, Song of Solomon

2nd Kings–2nd Chronicles-Lamentations

70-year exile in Babylon-Ezekiel and Daniel

Post exile

Ezra–Esther

Nehemiah

End of chronological order.

Post-exile prophets with Ezra and Nehemiah-Haggai, Zechariah, and Malachi

ISRAEL NORTH GODLESS 10 TRIBES PROPHETS

Amos, Hosea

JUDAH SOUTH 2 TRIBES PROPHETS

Joel, Micah, Isaiah, Zephaniah, Habakkuk, and Jeremiah

FOREIGN COUNTRY PROPHETS

Jonah, Nahum, and Obadiah

Acknowledgments

Father, Son, and Holy Spirit

Steve Shermett: Jewish Bible Teacher- for the chronological Old Testament.

Sarah Parkins: Editorial review from a reader's viewpoint.

For other books by Don Nordstrom, type his name into the search field at Amazon, Barnes and Noble, or other favorite book sellers. For questions or comments, please contact him at the email address below.

Email: thedesertpg@protonmail.com

www.ingramcontent.com/pod-product-compliance
Lightning Source LLC
Chambersburg PA
CBHW060527150626
46553CB00023B/604